DANCE MOVEMENT THERAPY

D0209438

CREATIVE THERAPIES IN PRACTICE

The *Creative Therapies in Practice* series, edited by Paul Wilkins, introduces and explores a range of arts therapies, providing trainees and practitioners alike with a comprehensive overview of theory and practice. Drawing on case material to demonstrate the methods and techniques involved, the books are lively and informative introductions to using the creative arts in therapeutic practice.

Books in the series:

Psychodrama
Paul Wilkins

DANCE MOVEMENT THERAPY

A Creative Psychotherapeutic Approach

Bonnie Meekums

SAGE Publications
London • Thousand Oaks • New Delhi

© Bonnie Meekums 2002

First published 2002

Apart from any fair dealing for the purposes of research or
private study, or criticism or review, as permitted under the
Copyright, Designs and Patents Act, 1988, this publication may
be reproduced, stored or transmitted in any form, or by any
means, only with the prior permission in writing of the
publishers, or in the case of reprographic reproduction, in
accordance with the terms of licencees issued by the Copyright
Licensing Agency. Inquiries concerning reproduction outside
those terms should be sent to the publishers.

 SAGE Publications Ltd
6 Bonhill Street
London EC2A 4PU

SAGE Publications Inc
2455 Teller Road
Thousand Oaks, California 91320

SAGE Publications India Pvt Ltd
32, M-Block Market
Greater Kailash – I
New Delhi 110 048

British Library Cataloguing in Publication data

A catalogue record for this book is available from the British
Library

ISBN 0 7619 5766 9
ISBN 0 7619 5767 7 (pbk)

Library of Congress Control Number: 2002102291

Typeset by Photoprint, Torquay, Devon
Printed in Great Britain by TJ International Ltd, Padstow,
Cornwall

To all my playmates, past and present,
and especially Jackie, Joseph, Rosa,
Philip and Cameron

CONTENTS

List of Figures and Tables

Figures

Tables

FOREWORD

Creativity shared by other arts therapies such as music, art, drama and poetry is the unique contribution of arts therapies – the creative process intrinsic to the relationship between therapist and client and the creative process of finding options of behaviour. This book is the first I have read that demonstrates clearly how creativity contributes to health and how the journey is often a joyful one.

My familiarity with the clinical and academic work of Dr Meekums began in the early 1980s. My greatest admiration for her came from observing her work with some of her clients in a treatment centre in northern England. These women received respectful and insightful attention, helping them to feel positive about themselves and enabling them to engender confidence in their children. Her writing contains the same characteristics.

Now, Dr Meekums' new book recalls the 1977 observation of Anthony Storr: 'The arts share with science the aim of seeking order in complexity and creating unity out of diversity'. For the reader, Dr Meekums' metaphoric use of a journey through the history and diversity of the field of dance movement therapy clarifies the concept and avoids unnecessary jargon. Along with the 'how' and 'why' of psychotherapy, Dr Meekums provides realistic examples of people whose lives have benefited from dance movement therapy.

An effort to address the emotional, cognitive and social trauma of human experience entails a complex mixing of neurological, social and emotional variants. Other professions addressing these complex factors have made remarkable progress in linking theoretical concepts to actual practice. Dance movement therapy, however, rests somewhat uncomfortably between the arts and sciences, drawing equally from each area yet still awaiting adequate linkage between diverse theoretical approaches, research findings from various disciplines and actual practice in the field. Dr Meekums accomplishes a new clarity within her field in this book.

It is my honour to recommend this book to psychotherapy practitioners.

Dianne Dulicai, PhD, ADTR
President, American Dance Therapy Association

PREFACE

This book has been great fun and scary all at once to write. The scary bit comes from knowing that nothing stands still. In committing myself to the written word I risk my practice becoming ossified in the minds of others. Words, I feel, are difficult and inadequate in this work. Despite the fact that I write with the benefit of many years' experience, if I were to write this book again in a few years time I hope that I would be saying things a little differently. Nevertheless, it has been a delight to me to be able to sum up where I have got to so far. In so doing, I have managed to contain some of the many books inside my head.

My hope is that, in committing myself to forming this volume, I will contribute in some small part to the development of DMT as both an academic and clinical discipline. Whether in agreement with me or in opposition to me, if the reader finds something here to stimulate their thinking, then I will have achieved that goal.

ACKNOWLEDGEMENTS

I wish to thank the series editor, Paul Wilkins, for his genuine interest in dance movement therapy and insightful comments concerning early versions of my manuscript, and Alison Poyner of Sage Publications for her helpful editorial suggestions.

In my development as a dance movement therapist, I owe much to my dance teachers Mary Fulkerson and Steve Paxton. Together they helped me to trust in my body's impulse to move and be still, whilst encouraging me to harness and train my movement potential.

The American dance movement therapists with whom I had contact in the 1980s helped me to see that I was not alone in what I was discovering about DMT. Joanna Harris, ADTR, provided a strong, clinically grounded approach and shared with me a passion for the work of D.W. Winnicott. Sharon Goodill, ADTR, validated my intuitive sense of the movement metaphor. And Dr Marcia Leventhal, ADTR, reaffirmed my sense that my own intuitive body movement contained the wisdom of insight.

Dianne Dulicai, ADTR, who has written the Foreword to this book, gave valuable support to my work with families and taught me much about observation of family systems. It is indeed a joy to work with her again, and to have my work witnessed by her in this altogether different way. The last time she did so was in person, travelling many miles within Britain to do so, meeting with me and seeing videotapes of my work with families and groups of mothers with young children. This time we have both travelled metaphorically across the pond, and Dianne has witnessed me through my words.

I want to thank all the pioneering employers who supported DMT in the UK in its early days, including John Cordon at Family Service Units, and John Casson and John Archer at Tameside Hospital.

My family has sustained me during my own development as a dance movement therapist. My children Joseph, Rosa and Cameron (some now grown) have moved inside me, danced with me, and tolerated their mother's seemingly whacky (pre)occupation. My husband Philip Spence, whose job is far more mainstream than mine, has never once been disparaging and has always been supportive of my chosen path. He has been a constant source of encouragement as I have wrestled with many ideas and inspirations, some of which have finally taken form in this book.

Without the many people who have been brave enough to try out the power of DMT for themselves, I would not have written this book. Many of my clients have generously consented to the anonymous use of case material from our work together, in order hopefully to bring alive the subject of DMT for the reader of this book. I have deliberately at times disguised this material by using composite details from more than one client. Nevertheless, all of the case material presented is based on actual clinical experience. Pseudonyms are used throughout this book.

ABBREVIATIONS

ADMT (UK) The Association for Dance Movement Therapy (UK)
ADTA   The American Dance Therapy Association
AM   Authentic Movement™
BMC   Body Mind Centering™
BPD   Borderline Personality Disorder
BRDMT   Basic Registered Dance Movement Therapist
CNS   Central Nervous System
CORE   Clinical Outcomes in Routine Evaluation
DMT   Dance Movement Therapy
EBP   Evidence Based Practice
LMA   Laban Movement Analysis
NHS   National Health Service (UK)
RCT   Randomised Controlled Trial
RDMT   Registered Dance Movement Therapist
SRDMT   Senior Registered Dance Movement Therapist
UKCP   United Kingdom Council for Psychotherapy

PART I
Mapping the Territory

1

THE REGIONAL MAP: AN OVERVIEW OF THIS BOOK

This book introduces the reader to Dance Movement Therapy (DMT) as a form of psychotherapy. I do this within the metaphor of a journey. Before we embark on any journey we need maps. The first part of the book therefore maps our territory. This chapter maps the book as a whole, and sets the book in context by giving an overview of DMT theory and practice. Chapter 2 offers a more detailed map of DMT theory. Theory gives us a way of understanding what DMT is and how it works. My dissatisfaction with the 'pasting on' of theories from other disciplines (usually verbal psychotherapy) has led me to re-examine DMT. I propose a unified theory of DMT, emphasising the creative process and in particular the role of the 'movement metaphor'.

In the second part of this book, I describe my particular approach to DMT practice. I organise this part around the idea of DMT as a creative process, with its four aspects of preparation, incubation, illumination and evaluation. I make use of extensive reference to case study material in order to illustrate each stage of the process.

In Chapter 3 I propose a 'containment' approach to DMT, suitable for the early preparation or 'warm-up' phase of each session and of the therapy as a whole, and for clients struggling with over-powering experiences. I then examine in Chapter 4 the role of DMT in allowing the process to deepen and in developing insight. This is the stage of confrontation with dungeons and dragons, a letting-go into the darkness (incubation) before seeing a crack of light (illumination). I end in Chapter 5 with a consideration of the role of DMT in processing and evaluating transitions, as we settle around the final campfire. At the end of the book are references and useful addresses, should you wish to explore further the topics raised in this book.

My case vignettes are all based on real experience, though some are presented as 'composite pictures' or with certain characteristics changed or disguised in order to protect confidentiality. Changes are only made where this does not affect the validity of the point being made. Pseudonyms are used throughout.

What is Dance Movement Therapy?

In Britain, DMT is defined as: 'the psychotherapeutic use of movement and dance through which a person can engage creatively in a process to further their emotional, cognitive, physical and social integration' (ADMT UK, 1977).

What is interesting about this definition is that it places DMT firmly within the realms of psychotherapy. For many years, mainstream psychotherapy in the UK was envisaged solely as a talking therapy, and psychoanalytic or at least psychodynamic in its orientation. With the advent of psychotherapy registration via the United Kingdom Council for Psychotherapy (UKCP) it has been possible to embrace all three of the major schools of psychotherapeutic thought (psychodynamic, behavioural and humanistic) and more. Nevertheless, the arts therapies (dramatherapy, art therapy, music therapy and DMT) are generally not represented within UKCP and maintain their own systems of registration.

Dance Movement Therapy or Therapeutic Dance?

One of the confusions that abounds in many people's minds concerns the overlap between therapeutic dance and dance movement therapy. A lot of very valuable work goes on in the area of therapeutic dance, and both professions are required in order to meet the varied needs of our society. However, it is worth attempting to delineate the differences and similarities.

Therapeutic dance may be practised by talented and highly skilled dance teachers who are not trained as therapists but work within institutions such as schools, prisons and so on. There is considerable overlap between DMT and therapeutic dance, giving rise to some fruitful cross-fertilisation. One important figure in the development of DMT in Britain has been the dance artist Wolfang Stange, who works with mixed groups of dancers including those with learning and physical disabilities. His goals are artistic; he runs a performance group, yet his methods look very similar to those used by dance movement therapists.

Both dance movement therapists and dancers working in therapeutic contexts are artists. Table 1.1 offers a comparison between the two disciplines. This is based both on my own practical experience and on the following sources: Boas (1943); Carnegie UK Trust (1985); Chace (1975); Claid (1977); Davidson (1979); Gill (1979); Hamilton (1989); Kestenberg and Sossin (1979); King (1983); Laban (1971); Leventhal (1986); Levy (1992); Malecka (1981); Meekums (1990); Meier (1997); Paludan (1977); Payne (1992); Prestidge (1982); Sherborne (c.1984); Solway (1988); Standing Committee of Arts Therapies Professions (1989); Stanton-Jones (1992); Steiner-Celebi (1996); Winnicott (1971). In reading my comparison, it is important to remember that this is an evolving field and that the parameters of each discipline are constantly changing. Table 1.1 should therefore be viewed as a snapshot in time.

Allied Approaches to DMT

Other approaches to movement and dance that may be seen as allied to DMT include:

- Body Mind Centering™ (BMC) (Cohen 1980, 1984), a complex training based on both developmental movement and anatomy. BMC is used both to support performance and as a system of therapy. Several British dance movement therapists have trained in BMC, but by no means all BMC practitioners have registration as dance movement therapists.
- Gabrielle Roth's five rhythms (flowing, staccato, chaos, lyrical, stillness), which she views as a form of shamanism (1990). As the name suggests, the work centres around five rhythmic structures within which the dancer improvises.
- Circle dance, based on folk dances from around the world and often deemed to hold archetypal, healing significance. I discuss their usefulness with survivors of child sexual abuse in my book *Creative Group Therapy for Women Survivors of Child Sexual Abuse* (2000). I have also encouraged some groups to choreograph their own 'circle dance', based on a given theme

Table 1.1 *Comparison of DMT and Therapeutic Dance*

Field	DMT	Therapeutic Dance
Facilitator is an artist	Yes	Yes
Boundaries	Start and finish times, group rules, private space, confidentiality, limits to relationship (no socialisation).	Start and finish times and privacy of space may be more relaxed. Group rules may be relaxed or strict. Relationships may extend beyond the group.
Use of structure offered by leader	Probably, but in response to therapeutic goals and client's own contribution. Likely to be flexible.	Probably. Not necessarily responsive to the client's contribution. May be rigidly adhered to, or flexible.
Use of props	Probably. May be used as 'transitional objects' (Winnicott, 1971).	Probably. Used to stimulate creativity.
Performance to outside audience	Unlikely	Possibly
Performance to other members of group	Possibly	Probably
Use of choreographic structures	Possibly	Possibly
Use of improvisational structures	Definitely	Probably
Use of rhythm	Yes. To structure and contain. Also to develop certain psychological/developmental states.	Yes. To structure and contain, and to develop skills.
Use of mirroring (rhythm, quality and shape of movement)	Yes. Conscious use to develop therapeutic relationship and group interrelationships.	Yes. May be used as a choreographic device or to develop group interrelationships.
Use of costume	Limited	Possibly
Use of theatre lighting	Unlikely	Possibly
Typical group size	1 to 8 or 10 individuals	4 to 30 or more individuals
Emphasis on aesthetic components	No	Possibly
Aims	Targeted to the therapeutic needs of the client group.	Broadly therapeutic and sometimes educational/artistic.

Table 1.1 *continued*

Field	DMT	Therapeutic Dance
Theoretical underpinnings	Include psychological theories.	May or may not include psychological theories.
Client groups	Just about anybody, but may be subject to assessment.	Just about anybody, but may be targeted.
Competencies required	Experience in facilitation of groups and range of movement styles. Additional competencies including ability to work with distress.	Experience in facilitation of groups and in the movement form offered.
Own therapy required	Yes	No
Clinical supervision required	Yes	No
Level of academic training required	Post-graduate diploma minimum	No formal qualifications required
Work with group dynamics and interpersonal relationships	Definitely	Probably
Work with the internal imagery and symbolism of clients	Definitely	Probably
Integration of spiritual components	Possibly	Possibly
Distress versus fun	Actively work with distress, but fun is allowed and used to balance. 'Rescuing' by therapist avoided.	May avoid distress and emphasise fun. Alternatively, facilitator may act as shaman, 'rescuing' through the use of self.
Verbal evaluation of sessions	Usually	Not necessarily
Use of touch between therapist and clients	Rare	Occurs as part of normal interaction
Diagnostic or psychological formulation based on movement observation	Yes	Not necessarily

like 'empowerment'. These dances, performed at the end of each session, become a container for the session's material and reaffirm a sense of connectedness before leaving the session.

Key Principles Underpinning DMT

Dance movement therapy rests on certain theoretical principles. These are:

- Body and mind interact, so that a change in movement will affect total functioning (Berrol, 1992; Stanton-Jones, 1992)
- Movement reflects personality (North, 1972; Stanton-Jones, 1992).
- The therapeutic relationship is mediated at least to some extent non-verbally, for example through the therapist mirroring the client's movement (Chaiklin and Schmais, 1979; Stanton-Jones, 1992)
- Movement contains a symbolic function and as such can be evidence of unconscious processes (Schmais, 1985; Stanton-Jones, 1992).
- Movement improvisation allows the client to experiment with new ways of being (Stanton-Jones, 1992).
- DMT allows for the recapitulation of early object relationships by virtue of the largely non-verbal mediation of the latter (Meekums, 1990; Trevarthen, 2001).

The Evolution of Dance Movement Therapy

Dance Movement Therapy has had a separate development in the UK from the American experience. Whilst there have been American influences, it is true to say that some of the seeds of British DMT were being sewn before any significant input from American dance movement therapists began in the late 1970s and 1980s.

There are records of dance being used for therapeutic purposes in Britain during the nineteenth century (Browne, 1837). By the 1940s, a definite dance therapy movement had begun, paralleling that in the US. However, dance therapy at that time was seen as distinct from psychotherapy and it was not until the 1970s that a second wave of DMT pioneers began to experiment with the psychotherapeutic applications of dance and movement. This second wave eventually gave birth to DMT as we know it today in the UK, and is more akin to American practice.

Dance movement therapy in the twenty-first century is practised flexibly, either as a primary intervention and therefore as a form of focal psychotherapy, or as a supportive, adjunctive therapy. The more creative, supportive and adjunctive function of DMT overlaps in form and function with 'therapeutic dance'.

Training and Registration of Dance Movement Therapists

Training in the UK is at post-graduate level, for two or more years. Some courses offer a post-graduate diploma and others offer Masters level training. Courses are accredited via the professional association, the Association for Dance Movement Therapy UK (ADMT UK). During training, all DMT students must be in personal therapy. Theoretical training spans several academic disciplines including psychology, psychotherapy, anatomy and physiology, and of course dance movement therapy. Practical training includes weekly attendance at a DMT process group, 200 hours of client contact and 200 hours of non-contact related work activity (note-taking, staff meetings and other related activity). Practice is supervised both in a group setting and individually.

In Britain, there are three tiers of registration for dance movement therapists. The first of these, Basic Registration (BRDMT) is for those who have recently completed a post-graduate training in DMT. BRDMT is essentially a probationary qualification. Within two years, a BRDMT has to apply for Registered status (RDMT), having completed extra hours of supervised practice.

Senior Registered Dance Movement Therapists (SRDMT) have demonstrated extra supervised practice and personal therapy and submitted a paper of publishable standard. They qualify for private practice, teaching and supervision of others. SRDMTs have effectively been in training for approximately seven years (two years post-graduate training, two years as a BRDMT and a further three years as RDMT). RDMTs have been in training for up to four years. All fully registered British Dance Movement Therapists have thus had a similar length of training to that of any registered psychotherapist.

At present British dance movement therapists do not have registration with one of the formal psychotherapy bodies (for example, UKCP). It may be that the future of the profession lies in acknowledging that there are two ways of practising DMT: the more creative, supportive and adjunctive work on the one hand

9

(for BRDMTs) and the practice of DMT as a primary psychotherapeutic intervention on the other (for RDMTs and SRDMTs). The latter could conceivably negotiate status as psychotherapists via UKCP. The stumbling block to such registration has been to date that many, but not all, dance movement therapists would wish to be seen as psychodynamically orientated. However, they would be unlikely to be afforded equal status with their counterparts in verbal psychodynamic psychotherapy. The UKCP has no separate category for arts therapists, although one member organisation trains its students in an integrative arts therapies approach and registers under the humanistic and integrative section.

Practice Contexts for DMT

Dance movement therapists in Britain work with a wide range of client groups. Many work in the National Health Service (NHS), usually in adult mental health. Others work in child and/or family services, both statutory and voluntary agency based. Some dance movement therapists work in social services, for example with adults who have learning disabilities. Other locations and client groups include prisons, education (with children who have emotional and behavioural disturbance) and private practice.

The Importance of Research

There is a strong and growing trend in Britain towards evidence based practice (EBP) within the NHS. This has been driven by a series of government initiatives and is broadly welcomed by the profession. It is important that clients and referrers can make informed choices wherever possible concerning treatment options. Most importantly, clients should not be offered a form of treatment that is unlikely to benefit or may even damage them.

The 'gold standard' for research is taken as the Randomised Controlled Trial (RCT). In this form of research, adapted from the natural sciences (physics, chemistry and biology), DMT is offered to one group of individuals (the 'experimental' group), and the same number of individuals is offered 'treatment as usual' (the 'control' group). The allocation to each of these two groups is random in an attempt to minimise researcher bias. A series of valid and reliable measures relating to the research question is used with both the experimental and control groups, at similar intervals, usually equating to before and after therapy. For example, if the research question is 'Does DMT reduce depression?' the measure will be a depression scale such as the Beck Depression Inventory (Beck, 1978). Statistical tests are then applied to the data to ascertain whether any difference in outcome between the two groups is deemed to be significant. A significant difference implies a causal relationship. For example, if the experimental group (those receiving DMT) show a statistically significant decrease in scores on the Beck Depression Inventory as compared to the control group (treatment as usual), it is considered likely that DMT has caused a reduction in depression in the experimental group.

Experimental research has demonstrated a role for DMT in reducing anxiety (Cruz and Sabers, 1998; Erwin-Grabner et al., 1999; Low and Ritter, 1998; Ritter and Low, 1996). As a form of gentle exercise, it is likely also that DMT has all of the positive health effects generally associated with this, including potentially the alleviation of depression (Ernst et al., 1998). However, there are fundamental problems with experimental methodology when applied to DMT research. It is often difficult to gather sufficient numbers to obtain a reliable result. The research is also limited by the measures available, so that it is difficult to investigate phenomena associated with complex symptom pictures or changes in beliefs, attitudes, feelings and relationships. Some research has focussed on the practice of developing DMT by participating with service users. This kind of research typically makes use of focus groups or conversational interviews and generates complex descriptive data rather than numerical data. Conclusions are likely to be similarly complex. For example, my own research (Meekums, 1998) showed that some women who had been sexually abused as children needed to use DMT in a very structured way in order to feel safe, while others benefited from the freedom of expression afforded through less structured, improvisatory forms. This difference seemed to be determined by the woman's degree of emotional and cognitive 'distance' from the abuse. Distance is a complex phenomenon that cannot be reduced to one single factor, for example length of time spent in treatment.

Navigating this Book

It is important not to skip the theory chapter of this book (Chapter 2), as this will help the reader to make sense of the practice of

2

THE DETAILED MAP: DMT AS A CREATIVE PSYCHOTHERAPY

Theoretical models for understanding and explaining dance movement therapy (DMT) abound, but many of them simply borrow from traditional psychotherapy theories normally associated with the 'talking therapies' (see, for example, Bernstein, 1986). These models can often be mistifyingly full of jargon. Attempts to develop a theory of DMT within existing psychotherapeutic models have severe limitations. DMT is not simply verbal psychotherapy with movement tacked on, nor is it dance or movement with verbal psychotherapy added. It is a form of psychotherapy in its own right.

In order to build a meaningful theory of DMT as a psychotherapy in its own right, we need to look more broadly at theories that have relevance. These include theories relating to: creativity, the body–mind relationship, nonverbal communication, interpersonal relationships and personal change. In this chapter I present my model of DMT as a creative act in which the central importance of the movement metaphor supersedes any emphasis on behavioural, cognitive, relational, spiritual or psychodynamic goals. The movement metaphor is the vehicle through which these goals can be effected, and is universally utilised in DMT practice. In the past, DMT theory has been defined by its goals and thus split. Practitioners have defined themselves as psychodynamic, behavioural, humanistic, transpersonal and so on. My emphasis on the movement metaphor, which I will illustrate throughout this book with case material drawn from a variety of contexts and therapeutic goals, enables DMT praxis to be understood within a unified theory of DMT as a distinct form of creative psychotherapy.

Dance Movement Therapy as a Creative Act

In any human change process something 'new' is being created. This 'newness' is often perceived as a transformation of old and outmoded patterns of behaviour, relating or thinking, like a phoenix rising from the ashes. In successful psychotherapy there is a sense that the 'self' has been changed in some way. Of course, this sense of a changed self is not unique to psychotherapy. It is common parlance to say 'I feel like a new man/woman' after something as simple as a good rest, or a shower and change of clothes. However, this kind of change is likely to be temporary (one shower won't do you for the whole of your life!). The changes achieved through psychotherapy (and certain other practices, including many spiritual practices) may potentially impact on the individual's core beliefs about the self and others, and about the world in general. This may result in a re-patterning of relationships, behaviours, emotions and cognitions. The core identity remains the same, but our 'take' on life may shift fundamentally. To use another analogy, it is as if the old tune has been rearranged, with fresh harmonies that soothe the soul.

The creative process in psychotherapy occurs within the relationship between client and therapist. The working aspect of this relationship can be conceptualised as existing within the 'potential space' between client and therapist, belonging to both of them (Winnicott, 1971). This is the place where the unconscious and conscious of both parties can co-exist, and it is also the area of play and creativity. The creative psychotherapeutic process thus mirrors early mother–infant processes. According to Winnicott, 'it is only in being creative that the individual discovers the self' (ibid., p. 63).

All creative acts, whether choreography, science or research (Meekums, 1993), occur within a recognisable creative process. This process is commonly considered to be cyclical with four stages: *preparation, incubation, illumination* and *evaluation* (Hadamard, 1954; Poincaré, 1982). The same four-stage process is also a feature of DMT and the other arts therapies (Blatt, 1991; Gordon, 1975; Meekums, 1998, 1999, 2000). The process is summarised in Figure 2.1.

The idea of a creative cycle is a workable model. It should never be confused with 'truth', which is deeply personal. Even the notion of a neat cycle is mere fiction, but as with any workable model it helps us to organise our own thoughts about the process. One

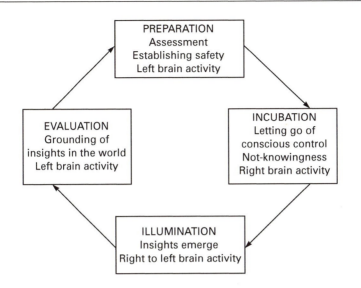

Figure 2.1   *The Creative Process in Therapy*

thing is almost certain: it is doubtful that therapy ever stops at just one 'cycle'. That is to say, there is more than one occasion during therapy, and sometimes several in any one therapy session, when illumination occurs and is evaluated. I prefer to see the process as a spiral. As we travel along the spiral, we pass the same images several times, but each time from a slightly elevated perspective. The result is increased clarity and an ability to see new gestalts.

The creative process depends on the capacity of the individual to both make use of and surrender the functions normally associated with ego (Gordon, 1975). There is a rhythmic interchange between action and quiet receptivity, between dream-like states and consciousness, between intuition and the world of the senses, between image and concretisation, between abandonment and control, between individual and shared reality. This rhythmic process mirrors the infant's engagement and disengagement with its mother[1] described by Stern (1977) and others (see below, and Meekums, 1993).

Preparation
The preparation phase of DMT in microcosm could be characterised by the warm-up phase of the session. In macrocosm, it corresponds to the earliest stage of therapy. The client arrives with

a history of having tried to grapple with life's problems, with varying degrees of success. The dance movement therapist may choose to take the client through a formal 'assessment' procedure, designed to find a focus for the work. Clients may be feeling apprehensive, wondering how they will feel about DMT, what they might uncover during therapy and also wondering whether it is possible or wise to trust the therapist to contain this within a genuinely human but professional therapeutic relationship.

Anne came to see me, and sat on the edge of her chair, wearing a large padded coat. Her body was turned towards the door. She did not at any stage in the session make eye contact. I concluded that this was enough working through her body for her for today. She seemed to be telling me how hard it was to trust me. She later revealed that her previous therapist had seen her for nearly a year before saying that he did not feel sufficiently skilled to hear her story. I felt her sense of having been dropped, of not having been 'held' properly.

As Rogers (1957) suggested, the successful therapeutic relationship is characterised by the therapist's unconditional positive regard for the client, empathic responses and congruence. Together, these factors help to establish the conditions of safety within the therapeutic relationship. The client's perception of safety within the therapeutic milieu is a *vector catalyst* to the therapeutic process (Meekums, 1998, 1999, 2000). In other words, if it is present it encourages the client's growth towards what Maslow (1999) called self-actualisation (becoming more fully who you really want to be), but when it is absent the therapy can be harmful.

Much of the therapeutic relationship is mediated non-verbally, although verbal responses are also important. Congruence, one of the necessary conditions for a positive therapeutic relationship (Rogers, 1957) is about 'being outwardly as you are inwardly – there is a harmony between internal process and outward behaviour' (Wilkins, personal communication, 2000). Therapists therefore need to be able to attend to their 'insides'. One useful system for teaching people to do this is Focusing™, also known as experiential psychotherapy. Focusing was developed by Eugene Gendlin (1981). He describes six 'movements' to the process: clearing a space, the felt sense, finding a handle, resonating the handle with the felt sense, asking, and receiving. Focusing emphasises the wisdom of the body, balanced with a judicious use of the intellect. The notion of the 'felt sense' has obvious relevance to dance movement therapists, but is also valued by some practitioners from other therapeutic approaches as seemingly diverse as person-centred therapy (Winter, personal communication, 2000) and cognitive therapy (Hackman, 1998).

Incubation

In the DMT session, this phase is often called 'process'. Having warmed up the body, spontaneous movements become more obviously expressive of the intrapsychic material of the individual and of the shared themes in the group. This is when the movement becomes metaphoric, that is it symbolises something for clients, whether or not they are consciously aware of its meaning. Metaphor is such an important aspect of DMT that I consider it separately below. I will also refer to the 'movement metaphor' in subsequent chapters, making use of case study material to illustrate the DMT process as a whole.

Geoffrey chose a prop to move with. He picked a black cloth, and after swirling it around above his head and at waist height for a while, he went over to the corner of the room, carefully picked out one of the floor cushions, and wrapped it tightly in the cloth.

In the above example, Geoffrey was clearly immersed (incubating) in his creative process, and engaging in a symbolic act. However, it was not yet clear, either to him or to me as his therapist, precisely what this symbolism was or where it could lead us.

In the therapy as a whole, incubation is only possible once trust in the therapist has been established. The beginning of symbolisation implies a willingness by the client to communicate personal and complex material to the therapist. However, the precise significance of this communication often remains unclear and unconscious. Developmentally, the therapeutic relationship at this stage might be said to mirror the merged state of mother and infant. At this early stage in the infant's life, communication between mother and infant is largely non-verbal. The infant depends totally on its mother (or primary caregiver) and has not yet learned to verbalise its needs or to manipulate its environment. In the therapeutic relationship mirroring this stage of infant development, the therapist or client may feel of 'stuck', as if waiting for some outside force to rescue them. The client may feel that only the therapist can 'make it better'. It is crucial in order for therapy to progress to the next stage that the therapist acknowledges in supervision any feelings either of omnipotence or of deskilling resulting from this powerful dynamic. Once these feelings are recognised by the therapist as part of a developmental sequence, it becomes possible to acknowledge the therapist's inability to 'make it better' and thus to empathically hand back the responsibility for change to the client, where it rightfully belongs.

In shamanistic and Jungian therapies, there is an acknowledgement during the incubation stage of therapy of what is often described as a descent by the client into symbolic 'death' (Lewis, 1988), or as a descent into the chaos of the unconscious (Kane, 1989). This can be disturbing or even frightening for the client, and is only possible when the conditions of safety have been firmly established within the therapeutic relationship and within the modality of dance movement therapy.

Whilst preparation is active, incubation has a quality of 'letting go'. There may be a sense of 'not knowing'. The artist (and therefore arts therapist) and mystic both share a capacity to let go of control (Gordon, 1975). They each acknowledge that something unknowable might exist, whether this is located inside or outside of the individual. A good dance movement therapist keeps intervention to a minimum at this point in the therapy, and simply 'holds the space', allowing the client to experience being alone in the presence of a benevolent other (Winnicott, 1958). It is important not to rush into a false sense of knowing. False knowledge is determined by previously learned patterns and lacks the quality of freshness that true insight brings. The therapist must be able to tolerate and even value periods of bewilderment and learn to 'fly by the seat of one's pants' in order to release the client from any compulsion to cling to the known and controllable. This release opens up possibilities for play and creativity of a kind normally only experienced by children and by those blessed souls who can consciously abandon themselves to seeing each leaf or hearing each birdsong or meeting each relationship afresh. Incubation is essentially a here-and-now experience, yet symbolically containing all time and all space (Meekums, 1993). Ultimately, this state might lead to a potentially spiritual sense of fusion and oneness as described by the dancer Mary Fulkerson (1987: 20):

It's a genuine feeling state of, I would call it, emptiness or wholeness, or oneness, or stillness. It's a kind of place from which the world can be considered, and so through being in and with the stillness, I can look at events or see things happen or play with extreme imagination, anything, knowing that there's this anchor, or this place, this sort of still pool, a great presence underneath.

Illumination

Illumination is the stage in the session at which meanings become apparent. However, rather than a straightforward transition from one to the other, there is often an oscillation between this and incubation. Rather like the resonance described by Gendlin (1981), between the 'felt sense' (a state of unclarity) and the 'handle' (a state of relative clarity), it is as if the raw physical expression of emotion during incubation (a right brain activity) resonates with the sense-making of illumination (a linked right and left brain activity). Illumination can involve dramatic revelations for the client about the meaning of either their movements, their internalised, kinaesthetic imaging, or old patterns of behaviour. This can be exciting or distressing.

Gary was part of a group that had been tossing a ball up and down on a piece of stretched cloth. Suddenly, I noticed that Gary seemed to be becoming distressed. I asked him what he was feeling, and he said that he had felt like the ball as a child, tossed around between his fighting parents.

On the other hand, illumination may be more subtle and cumulative, only perceived with hindsight.

Linda had been a professional dancer. For her, dance was from an early age a refuge from the outside world. When life got tough, she got going. She would go into the studio and dance out her pain and her rage, turning pirouette after pirouette and leaping high into the air. She also found that she could exert some control in her life by eating a strict diet and dancing in a way that denied her body's needs for rest and nourishment. When she came to me for DMT, she was surprised to find that for the first time dance was not a refuge. For the first time, she was being asked to LISTEN to her body, to be still until the impulse came to move. She reacted to this suggestion with fury and superiority, claiming that this was not real dance. We worked together for a few months, but it seemed to me like an uphill struggle. I felt dismissed by her. I realised in supervision that I felt the way her body did! Years later, on a chance meeting, she told me that she had since been to see a Gestalt psychotherapist who had also encouraged her to listen to her body. She said that her work with me had been the impetus for her to seek further help. She was still dancing, but was now performing her own work, 'dancing to her own tune' and studying more gentle forms of dance and movement.

The moment of illumination marks the beginning of the separation of the individual from the merged state experienced during incubation, during which the individual's impulses were not linked to understanding and thus lacked form. Whilst mystics undoubtedly achieve moments of insight, it is the urge to form, to separate although painful from the 'great presence' (Fulkerson, 1987) experienced during incubation that marks the difference between the artist and the mystic (Gordon, 1975). In the DMT process, the client is like the artist. There is an urge to form, to understand, to make sense of what is happening. This is accompanied by a shift in perspective (Meekums, 2000) which can fundamentally alter the client's world view and thus their sense of self.

In the therapy as a whole, illumination may include a reappraisal of experience, a sense that a corner has been turned. Developmentally, the therapeutic relationship has almost 'grown up' and the client is ready to contemplate an ending.

Evaluation
Evaluation is an active state, making full use of conscious, rational 'left brain' activity, though not without reference to the body. In this stage of the session, client and therapist may discuss together the significance of the therapeutic process in the client's life. This is essentially a 'grounding' process. Therapy should never be an end in itself; there is always a purpose in the real world. Evaluation involves relating what was learned in today's session and in the therapy as a whole to the client's life outside the therapy room. The client may spontaneously make resolutions, like spending more time with the children or reading a good book that was previously longed for but denied.

Sandra and I were throwing the ball back and forth to each other. When Sandra told me that the ball felt like it was in her face, just as she often experienced friends and family in this way, I told her that I had noticed she was throwing it over- arm. I wondered what would happen if she threw it under- arm? She tried this out, and said that she had a much clearer view of everything. I also noticed that her musculature had relaxed and she seemed more in control of the ball. I fed this information back to her. She checked this for herself and decided that this was so. We then discussed what this met- aphor would mean if she translated it into her everyday life. She realised she was being engulfed by the problems of her extended family and that she needed to take steps to prevent this happening, to achieve more of a balance between her own needs and those of the people she loved. She decided to make the problems of others less central to her vision by assessing the personal cost of each demand made upon her, and some- times saying no. She had maintained that shift when I saw her for a follow-up appointment after her therapy had ended.

In the Evaluation phase of the therapy as a whole, the client will prepare for an ending with the therapist. This may include a formal 'review' of the therapy, looking back over the time spent together and evaluating this in the light of previous difficulties and tasks for the future. There may be a focus in sessions on present-day issues. For example, a client who came to therapy to work on her feelings about her body may find that she now wants to celebrate her new body image and relate this change to previous concerns about her relationship with her partner.

Evaluation may perhaps more rightly be called 'grounding', as it is essentially a process of n   al or of embodying the insights gained in the previou   975: 5) highlights the pain involved in such em

the element of sacrifice which inexor of limits and limitations that impose themselves idea, the ideal, the spirit is given form, body.

Movement Metaphor: the Central Tool of DMT

Whilst the creative process is a useful way to understand the process as a whole in DMT, movement metaphor is the essential tool used by dance movement therapists as the mediator of that process. Dance movement therapy is one of the arts therapies. In the UK, there are four recognised arts therapies: Dance Movement Therapy, Dramatherapy, Music Therapy and Art Therapy. Each of these has a distinct training and its own system of professional registration. Despite the central role of metaphor within the arts therapies as a whole (Gorelick, 1989), and despite the considerable literature on metaphor, very little has been written about the specific role of movement metaphor in DMT. Schmais (1985) bemoans the fact, a point later taken up by Stanton-Jones (1992), and Webster (1991) devotes a short chapter to the topic. However, these attempts fall short of using movement metaphor to delineate a clear and integrated theory or DMT.

A metaphor is the 'application of name or descriptive term to an object to which it is not literally applicable' (*Concise Oxford Dictionary*, third edition, 1964). This literary definition can be expanded to include not just words but visual images and body movements (Lakoff and Johnson, 1980). The word 'metaphor' comes from the Greek words *meta* and *phora*, meaning to carry across (Cox and Theilgaard, 1987).

The English language is littered with verbal metaphors that have somatic counterparts. One example is the reference to 'feeling low'. The tendency when feeling emotionally low is to adopt a low or sunken posture. Other movement metaphors, like 'being in a spin', may not be literally played out in the body, but if you were to try spinning very fast right now you would probably end up with some of the somatic symptoms experienced by the person who describes their state in this way. In the Disney/Pixar film *A Bug's Life*, Hopper's brother (a grasshopper) literally jumps out of his skin when he sees the previously docile bugs advancing menacingly towards him. When I saw the film, the meaning of this metaphor was clear, even to the four-year-old sitting next to me. He laughed, but did not question. It did not need explanation. I found the metaphor intriguing, having heard so many of my clients speak of their experiences of leaving the body during the experience of sexual abuse. It seems that such out-of-body experiences, developed as a response to trauma, are embodied in the metaphor of 'jumping out of one's skin'.

The movement metaphor is a symbol encapsulated in either a movement or posture. For example, a person may adopt a hunched posture (movement metaphor) when describing the 'burden' (verbal metaphor) they carry in life (Silberman-Deihl and Komisaruk,

1985). The movement metaphor exists in the creative space between client and therapist, mediating between the 'symbolic realm' of unconscious material and the 'knowing realm' of conscious awareness (Ellis, 2001), in other words between right and left hemispheres of the brain (Cox and Theilgaard, 1987). Both the therapist's and client's mutually influencing meanings and action lie at the interface between these 'knowing' and 'symbolic' realms.

Patrick considered himself to be a strong man. He held down a responsible job, requiring authority. However, a traumatic incident at work in which his life had been threatened forced him to revise his view of himself. He had reacted by feeling himself to be weak and 'spineless'. When we held two garden sticks between our hands and moved around the room together, he seemed to be backing himself into a corner. I noticed that the pressure between our hands was being taken by his upper body, without being connected into the pelvis and legs. As a result, he seemed to 'break' in the spine, at waist level. I fed this observation back to him, without mentioning the potential association with his view of himself as 'spineless'. Instead, we worked at a physical level to integrate his movements. As a result, he developed more balance and co-ordination and learned to deal with a certain degree of pressure without 'crumbling'. It was only much later that he was able to make the connection between the movement we had done together and his new-found view of himself, that he was basically strong but like everyone else had his limitations.

Movement metaphors can thus be seen as a form of nonverbal communication which, when examined, can provide valuable insights into the individual's patterns of behaviour, beliefs and relationships.

Metaphor is a form of symbolization. As such, it requires an 'as if' attitude, different from symbolic equivalence (Gordon, 1975). The latter implies more of a merging between symbol and the object symbolized, whilst symbolization recognises the separateness of the symbol and the thing it symbolizes. The earliest examples of the human capacity to symbolize exist in the child's use of transitional objects (like teddy bears and comfort blankets) and transitional phenomena (including symbolic movements like thumb sucking) (Winnicott, 1971). They provide a bridge between the individual and the merged state, and between inner and outer worlds. They exist in the 'potential space' between mother and infant, an area of shared creativity in which the self is discovered and developed. In DMT, the movement metaphor exists in the potential space between client and therapist.

To summarise, metaphor has the following qualities:

- Metaphor contains images that have sensory references (Billow, 1977).
- Metaphor can provide a way of working with a 'stuck' situation (Jones, 1996).
- Metaphor may aid memory by mediating between associative connections (Angus and Rennie, 1989; Billow, 1977).
- Metaphor reflects issues of self-identity (Angus and Rennie, 1989).
- Metaphor can provide a representation of role-relationship patterns used by the client (Angus and Rennie, 1989).
- Metaphor connects both with past experience and the potential to affect the future by creating a new reality (Lakoff and Johnson, 1980).
- Metaphor holds multiple meanings and contexts (Billow, 1977).
- Metaphor can function as a way of expressing something which might otherwise be inexpressible (Sledge, 1977).
- Metaphor provides economy of expression without losing richness, thus making an experience understandable to others (Billow, 1977).
- Metaphor bridges left brain and right brain activity, or conscious and unconscious processes (Cox and Theilgaard, 1987).
- Metaphor can lead to increased intellectual clarity (Billow, 1977).
- Metaphor can be used to explore alternative ways of thinking and behaving (Lakoff and Johnson, 1980).
- Metaphor can act both to distance the client from the emotional content of its reference, and to reduce the distance between client and therapist (Angus and Rennie, 1989; Cox and Theilgaard, 1987; Sledge 1977).
- It is not always necessary to proceed from metaphor to linguistic or conscious processing, and to do say may even reduce its therapeutic value (Chaiklin and Schmais, 1979; Grenadier, 1995; Shuttleworth, 1985).

- By using metaphor, one can create a new concept for which there is no other expression (Billow, 1977).
- Metaphor allows for serious and uncomfortable subjects to be explored, sometimes even with humour (Shuttleworth, 1985).
- It has been suggested that it is more difficult for people who are either brain damaged or suffering from schizophrenia to access metaphor than for the rest of the population (Billow, 1977). My own clinical experience is that metaphoric communication is both rich and meaningful for people who are in acutely psychotic states. It is possible that some, but by no means all, sites of brain damage affect the individual's capacity to work with metaphor.

Metaphor, because of its capacity both for holding many layers of complex meaning and for mutation of these meanings, is an ideal medium for exploration in therapy. This is particularly true for any therapy that acknowledges the individual constructionist and co-constructionist aspects of meaning. I have known, for example, cognitive behavioural therapists, systemic family therapists, psychodynamic psychotherapists and arts therapists all to make extensive use of metaphor. However, with the exception of arts therapists, metaphor is not universally seen as the theoretical underpinning of any of these psychological therapies.

The movement metaphor in DMT facilitates a complex interplay between the embodied experience of movement, associated sensori-motor 'body' memory, projected symbolism through the use of props, iconic imagery, affect and verbalisation. As such, it involves integration of the intuitive, affective right-brain functions and the logical, linguistic left-brain functions.

Stewart's breathing was shallow, his movements restricted, and his voice monotone. His whole body seemed to be telling me what he also said verbally during the assessment process: 'The less noise I make, the less I move, the better it will be'. Together we worked out that he had developed this coping strategy in response to childhood abuse. It had served him well at the time. He described vivid pictures in his mind of this abuse, accompanied by somatic symptoms associated with anxiety (including heart racing and dizziness). Stewart's passivity was becoming a problem for him. About half way through Stewart's therapy, we moved together using a large piece of cloth. We each held one end of the cloth, and I followed his lead as we wafted it up and down. He remarked that it was 'like a breath of fresh air'. As he observed this, he sighed deeply, as if allowing the breath into his body. I noticed that today he was moving much more freely than in previous sessions. We were able to link this shift to his descriptions of recent changes in his relationships within his family, which included a supportive stay with relatives in the country.

Movement Metaphor and Body Memory

Freud described the ego as first and foremost a body ego (Stanton-Jones, 1992). However, Winnicott made the important point that the body ego is based on bodily *experiences*. Through the mother's holding, the infant learns that it has a skin, the limits of which define 'me' and 'not me' (Winnicott, 1960a). This allows for concepts like 'inside of me'. The body thus becomes equated with the self.

The infant who does not receive adequate maternal holding may experience one of four 'unthinkable anxieties' (Winnicott, 1962). These are:

● going to pieces;
● falling forever;
● having no relationship to the body; and
● having no orientation.

These are essentially body or movement metaphors and as such may become manifest in the body movement and posture of the individual. For example, Patrick's 'break' in the spine, described above, seemed to reflect his sense that he had 'gone to pieces'. One of my clients had to lie on the floor when he became anxious, which seemed to be about a fear of 'falling'. As described above, some children learn during abusive experiences to dissociate from their bodies to the extent that they experience a sensation of floating on the ceiling, looking down on what is happening ('having no relationship to the body'). Another of my clients, though sighted, would cut off from visual cues by dropping her head. In movement improvisation, she would close her eyes and wander around the room in a floaty, aimless way. She had dropped out of college and had no idea what she might do next. She literally had no 'orientation'.

Justification for the notion that there is such a thing as 'body memory' is often drawn from the work of Wilhelm Reich, who suggested that emotions are repressed in the body in the form of what he called 'armouring' (1962). Armouring is noticeable in chronically held body tensions. It is as if whole body tension is an attempt to 'keep the self together'. Conversely, tension in one part of the body may be an attempt to 'cut off' from affect laden sensation in the distal body part.

Suzanne hated her legs. They were often bruised, as she found herself knocking them frequently. She disliked their shape intensely. When trying to give her weight to a large physiotherapy ball she fell off, because her legs were tense, thus raising her centre of gravity. Eventually, it occurred to me that she was ignoring, judging and comparing her legs unfavourably, just as she was ignored, judged and compared unfavourably against her siblings in her family of origin.

Further evidence for the movement metaphor as body memory lies in the study of neuroscience. All sensory information is processed via the central nervous system (CNS), made up of the brain and the spinal cord. For example, the eyes pick up patterns of light that are registered on the retina and information subsequently travels along the optic nerve to the brain. Kinaesthetic information from the joints and muscles travels along nerves to the spinal cord. For every sensory nerve connecting to the CNS, there is a corresponding motor nerve. Thus, for every sensory impulse there is also a motor impulse.[2] It follows that, for every sensory input we have ever experienced we have had a motor response, *even if we did not actually move.*

Some motor responses are automatic, but many can be slowed or inhibited by use of the cerebral cortex. The cortex is that part of the brain associated with mammals and includes the functions we call thinking, or cognition. Conscious thought is sophisticated in humans. However, cognition without affect does not lead to intelligent decision making (Turnbull, 2001). People who have lesions in the ventro-mesial frontal lobes (damage to the front of the brain which may occur, for example, after a motor bike accident) may be of normal intelligence but make bad life decisions. This part of the brain is associated with processing of affect (emotion). People with lesions in the ventro-mesial frontal lobes register emotion but are unable to learn from it and are no longer recognisably like their old selves (Turnbull, 2001). The loss of frontal lobe function is also associated with the loss of self-control (Solms, 1999). If a ventro-mesial frontal lobe lesion occurs under two years of age, the growing individual not only makes bad life choices but also lacks empathy, suggesting that this part of the brain is important in the development of empathy (Turnbull, 2001). It is thus a crucial area of the brain for interpersonal interactions, and for coping with stress (Schore, 1994).

We 'learn' as infants that when we hear a certain voice or see Mummy's face it means 'Mummy is here'. The feeling is one of pleasurable anticipation (hopefully), excitement, and often an urgent 'I want'. The accompanying motor response will probably include vigorous kicking of the legs, tracking of the mother's voice and accompanying vocalisation. Thus, the memory becomes a 'body memory' as a sensori-motor event, to which affect-laden meaning is attached.

Schore (1994, 2001) has shown that the right orbito-frontal cortex develops critically during the second year of an infant's life, in response to affectively charged sensori-motor interactions with the primary caregiver. The caregiver's responses to the infant are crucial in the development of this part of the brain. If the caregiver is neglecting or over-stimulating, the brain does not develop as it should. Infant–caregiver interactions become effectively 'hard wired' into the brain. They become patterned not simply as learned responses but as neurological pathways. Changes in the hard-wiring due to maladaptive parenting can result for the child later in life in a tendency towards depression, psychosomatic illness, difficulties with relationships and poor affect regulation with poor impulse control.

Early mother–child interactions are mediated non-verbally (Schore, 1994; Trevarthen 2001). One of the premises on which DMT operates is that, certain motor patterns contain a metaphoric significance. The metaphor acts as a link between sensori-motor experience, affect and cognition. Schore (1994) points out that early attachment experiences are associated with the movements of moving towards, moving away from and moving against. Whilst we may not consciously make these movements in relation to others, their significance is encoded in our language. We talk about 'getting close to someone', 'locking horns' or 'needing some space', for example. Repetition of these patterns in movement allows us to re-member (re-embody) the original meaning we attached to them. When this occurs within the laboratory of an attuned non-verbal therapeutic relationship, reprogramming of early psychobiological patterns may be possible (Schore, 1994).

Movement Metaphor and Body Language

Most of us learn from a very early age to read the body language of others. For example, if when I know my friend to be a generous hugger and then next time I see her I feel her body stiffen as I go to hug her, I know something is 'wrong' between us. Since the 1960s, some writers have been developing a more formal understanding of body language in relation to interpersonal communication (see, for example, Argyle, 1967, 1990). Research in this area has shown, for example, that two people who are 'in synch' with each other will synchronise to and mirror each other's shifts in posture (Scheflen, 1964). Even a newborn baby will synchronise its movements to the mother's speech pattern (Condon and Sander, 1974). This sense of being 'in synch' is observable neurologically in monkeys. When one monkey sees another monkey performing an action, the observing monkey's motor neurones fire as if performing the same action (Solms, 1999).

Dance movement therapists use a complex system of movement observation in order to understand the body language of their clients. Much of this is based on the work of the extraordinary choreographer, Rudolph Laban (1971), and on developments of his work by Warren Lamb (1965; Lamb and Watson, 1979), Marion North (1972), Judith Kestenberg (Kestenberg and Sossin, 1979) and Irmgaard Bartenieff (1980). Together, these form the basis of Laban Movement Analysis (LMA).

It is beyond the scope of this book to do more than sketch an outline of LMA. LMA focuses on three main areas of observation: body, effort and shape/space (Moore and Yamamoto, 1988). Aspects relating to the body include the individual's use of 'kinesphere' or reach space. We all know confident individuals who sweep into the room and seem to take up more space than their size would suggest. Such people would probably be described by a dance movement therapist as having a large kinesphere. Conversely, the kinesphere may be small in depressed individuals who find it hard to reach out to others. Of course, our kinespheres vary according to our mood and to the context.

Another aspect of the body is seen in the individual's relationship to the ground. For one man the ground was a safe place to be, to the extent that he would lie down when feeling panicky. A second individual felt the ground to be very unsafe. If she were to lie down she felt she could be raped or otherwise attacked. It is important to remember these sharp variations in preference when structuring DMT sessions, so that participants are not forced into places that they perceive to be unsafe.

Efforts are the motion factors relating to Weight (or force), Space, Time and Flow. These motion factors can either be indulged in (light Weight, flexible use of Space, sustained use of Time, and free Flow) or fought (strong Force, direct use of Space, sudden or accelerating use of Time, and a resistance or bound Flow). Each Effort element relates to a different function. Space is related to the function of attention. For example, my attention may wander off all over the place (indirect or flexible, indulging attitude to Space), or I might be very focussed and direct (fighting attitude to Space). Time relates to decision making. For example, I may be quite quick at making decisions (fighting attitude to Time), or I may need to take my time (indulging attitude to Time). My use of Weight or Force expresses my intention. In essence, this is the impact I make. I may be rather 'heavy handed' (fighting attitude to Weight) or tread lightly (indulging attitude to Weight). Flow is about emotion and relationship. The use of Flow can be seen in the breath and in the musculature. My example above, of the old friend who was holding back from hugging me, was using bound Flow (fighting attitude to Flow). On the other hand, when my small son runs into my arms with a big, broad smile and no-holds-barred he is using free Flow (indulging attitude to Flow).

LMA training does not always emphasise the importance of the movement metaphor. However, it is not difficult to see that each of the Effort elements is linked to a movement metaphor: 'being direct/indirect'; 'quick to jump to conclusions'/'taking his time'; 'throwing her weight about/treading carefully'; 'holding back/going with the flow'. The dance movement therapist can enhance awareness of the client's metaphoric communication through the use of 'kinaesthetic empathy' (Moore and Yamamoto, 1988). This is the process through which our own muscles respond to movement with which we are visually and empathically engaged, as if we were performing the same actions as we see. By tuning into how the movement feels in our own bodies, we can thus become more aware of what is being communicated.

The psychiatrist and psychoanalyst Judith Kestenberg (Kestenberg and Sossin, 1979) has identified separate rhythmic structures for the use of Flow, each rhythm corresponding to a stage of psychosexual development. For example, the oral libidinal rhythm is associated with the need for comfort and holding. We see this rhythm in the infant's sucking and in the soulful rocking of one who is bereaved. The oral sadistic rhythm is associated with biting, and may be seen in irritated tapping of the fingers on a desk when it tends to indicate a wish to cut things short and get away from either the person or the subject. Urethral rhythms are associated with impulse control and the stop-go games of the toddler. Anal rhythms are seen in breath holding and sighing, or in the wringing of hands. Inner genital rhythms are typical of a slow sway to blues music, and phallic rhythms are of course prevalent in sexual intercourse but also in swinging, skipping and leaping for joy. I have also seen them substitute for gentle rocking rhythms in families that found it difficult to nurture and soothe, with the result that children were often 'wound up' by their parents and each other, leading first to excitement and then to conflict.

Movement, like music, can be said to occur in 'phrases' or sequences. The phrasing of the individual's movement can be either impulsive (with the emphasis at the beginning of the phrase), impactive (with the emphasis at the end of the phrase) or swing (with a repeated alternation between fighting and indulging Efforts) (Bartenieff, 1980). Impulsive phrasing, for example, can often be seen in individuals who have difficulty in containing their aggressive impulses.

Finally, Shape, which is the specific contribution of Lamb (1965), shows the affinities between Effort qualities and the use of space around the body. The individual's attitude to Shape can be seen in Shape Flow, Directionality or Sculpting. Shape Flow is associated with early developmental patterns and is evident in the breath. It is characterised by a rhythmic opening and closing as in breathing in and out, and has an affinity to the Flow Effort. Closing is associated with Bound Flow, and Opening with Free Flow. Directional movement is goal orientated, forming bridges with the environment. Here we see: Upward with its affinity to Light Weight, as in reaching for an apple; Downward with an affinity to Strong Weight, as in pushing down on a case to close it; Forward with an affinity to Sustainment, as in creeping up on some-one; Backward with an affinity to Suddenness, as in a retreat from a shocking image; Widening with an affinity to Flexible use of Space, as in a curtain call; and Narrowing with an affinity to Direct use of Space as in fine needlework. Sculpting is associated with forming or adapting to the environment. It has a three-dimensional quality, as in an embrace or in kneading dough.

Table 2.1 summarises the Effort/shape affinities and their psychological correlates. Despite the usefulness of systems like LMA,

Table 2.1   *Effort/shape Affinities*

Effort	Shape	Psychological function
Flow	Open/close	Emotion and relationship
Time	Forward/backward	Decision
Space	Widen/narrow	Attention
Weight	Upward/downward	Intention

any system of observation should be used with caution and checked through other means. For example, certain uses of Effort and Shape are culturally determined or context-driven (Argyle, 1990). Sometimes there is no hidden symbolic significance to movement. I recall one occasion when interviewing a woman for the first time. She repeatedly leaned forward whenever I spoke. My co-worker remarked on this privately to me afterwards, and wondered what it meant. It turned out that this particular woman was partially deaf. Her leaning forward had been purely functional, in order to hear me better.

It is vital that dance movement therapists do not lose sight of the creative aspects of observation. This means not just 'analysing' the movement intellectually, but also accessing an intuitive sense of the person through metaphoric description. The dance movement therapist uses their kinaesthetic responses to help and guide this process. The combined intuitive, metaphorical and intellectual analysis is checked and refined in collaboration with the client.

Dance movement therapists, in their efforts to distance themselves from value judgements about their clients' dance, have rightly rejected aesthetic goals in the work. However, in so doing we risk losing the ability to value and reflect beauty in our clients' moments of transcendence and authenticity. I have been touched by the beauty of a mother and child engrossed in dancing together just as much, and felt just as satisfied as when watching a well choreographed ballet danced with extreme sensitivity.

Movement Metaphor and the Therapeutic Relationship

One of the key tasks of the dance movement therapist is to metaphorically hold and contain the client's experience, echoing but not precisely replicating a mother's holding and containment of her infant's experience.

The mother–infant relationship is mediated through eye contact, rhythm, sound, reciprocity, synchrony and sensori-motor experience including holding (Condon and Sander, 1974; Kestenberg and Buelte, 1977; Kestenberg and Sossin, 1979; Schaffer, 1977; Stern, 1971; Trevarthen, 2001; Winnicott, 1960a). The mother responds through mirroring, modifying or elaborating the child's movements and sounds. She also crucially knows when to be quiet and cease to stimulate (Brazelton et al., 1974; Fogel, 1977; Ostrov, 1981; Schaffer, 1977; Winnicott, 1960a). The rhythmic engagement and disengagement experienced in a healthy mother–infant relationship and framed by the mother's attention to her infant's needs becomes a blueprint for the later ability to work and relax, to relate and to be alone (Brazelton et al., 1974; Stern, 1977; Winnicott, 1958).

Mother and baby move and sing together in a way that indicates temporal coherence. It has been said that 'the mother sings, the baby dances' (Trevarthen, 2001). Such creative interactions build a sense for the infant that the world is responding in predictable patterns. The mirroring provided by the mother enables the infant to develop meanings as part of a co-created universe. The child's growing sense of self thus does not exist in isolation but in relationship (Balbernie, 2001).

The sense of being acknowledged and delighted in by the mother provides the baby with a sense of self, of pride and of self-esteem (Trevarthen, 2001). Shame, on the other hand, is the anticipation of loss of love and therefore akin to separation distress (Watt, 2001). Separation from a loved one is experienced as painful and spoken about using the metaphor of pain.

It has been noted that one of the roles of the mother is to modulate the baby's emotional state through her responses. The development of empathy and emotional self-regulation in the growing individual is only possible through the process of the mother's recognition of her infant's emotional state, which fires certain neuronal connections in the brain (Balbernie, 2001). Over time, this 'hard-wires' the brain due to the principle that 'neurones that fire together wire together' (Balbernie, 2001; Schore, 2001). It is literally a case of 'use it or lose it', the most crucial period being the first 18–36 months of life. Psychotherapists, though, remain hopeful that although the brain's plasticity is severely limited in adulthood, patterns laid down during this largely pre-verbal period can be modified right up to the end of life (Glaser, 2001).

The metaphor of 'internalisation' of the mother often spoken about within the world of psychotherapy is thus a real, neurological event. It follows that key emotional states associated with attachment and separation will become themes of any therapy and also the substrate of the therapeutic relationship. The dance movement therapist mirrors, then clarifies, elaborates or modifies the movements of her client. The therapist's movements and vocalisations respond both rhythmically, three-dimensionally and qualitatively to those of the client. The patience of the dance movement therapist is crucial, as discussed above. Whilst engaging in this relationship-forming activity, it is necessary to tolerate uncertainty during the incubation phase of the session and avoid stepping in to create false, premature insight, or over-stimulating the client when deep in a process. The similarity in function between the dance movement therapy relationship and the mother–infant relationship may lead the client to respond to the therapist as if she or he were playing one of the reciprocal roles in the client's internal world (Ryle, 1990). For example, the therapist may be perceived as an idealised caregiver, or even as an abusive figure. This phenomenon is sometimes referred to as transference. Cox and Theilgaard (1997), citing Pedder (1979), note that the meaning of the word transference, which derives from the Latin *trans* and *fereo*, is identical to that of metaphor, deriving from the Greek *meta* and *phora*. They both mean 'to carry across'.

The reciprocal role is experienced by the therapist as what is usually termed countertransference. In dance movement therapy (and in some other forms of psychotherapy), it is acknowledged that this can be experienced as a 'somatic countertransference' (Lewis, 1984), played out either through the dance itself and/or in physical sensations with or without any obvious emotional or attitudinal link. It is important for these to be processed in clinical supervision in order to understand them more fully, and therefore to understand the client. In groups, the therapist experiences this somatic countertransference as a response to what Jung called the 'collective unconscious' (Jung, 1990) of the group as a whole. In fact, the term 'somatic countertransference' refers not only to reciprocal role experiences, but also to role identification or what in the person-centred tradition is called empathy (Wilkins, personal communication 2000), as the following example demonstrates.

As I danced with the group, I felt heavy in my body, as if I wanted to sleep. I knew I had had enough sleep and had felt fine until we started to move, so I guessed this must be something to do with the group's process. I knew from experience that feeling sleepy was usually associated with a wish to escape. When I wondered aloud how the group members were feeling today, I noticed that I suddenly felt more alive. One by one it emerged that each member of the group had been feeling resistant this morning, due to underlying anger about certain aspects of their lives. We were then able to dance our struggle with that resistance, using the symbolism of collective warriors on a hero's journey, to overcome or come to terms with the obstacles in each individual's life.

Movement Metaphor and the Spiritual Dimension

There is an argument for the view that DMT contains a 'spiritual' or transpersonal dimension. Much of this has been described in terms of an 'unconscious link' (Lewis, 1988: 313) between the client and therapist, often expressed in the language of archetypes (Jung, 1990; Chodorow, 1991).

Examples of archetypal emotions include: the void of sadness, the abyss of terror, the chaos of rage, the alienation of contempt or shame (Chodorow, 1991). Each of these images has a counterpart. So, if the conscious affect is the void of sadness, the unconscious contains the counterpart of the beauty of nature. Similarly, the abyss is balanced by the holy mountain, chaos by the ordered cosmos, and alienation by utopian *communitas*. These balancing forces represent the 'fully embodied, integrated sense of Self as it evolves out of the primordial depths toward the highest aspirations of the human spirit' (Chodorow, 1991: 93).

Authentic Movement™ (AM), whilst not strictly speaking DMT, has influenced many DMT practitioners. It does not rely on any set movements, but instead encourages the dancer to move from within, in the presence of a witness or witnesses. Derived from Jungian concepts, AM allows the 'embodiment of the collective' (Adler, 1996: 84). This process is seen as necessary because 'we cannot endure the pain, the isolation, the despair of the separateness, from our own spirit, and from each other' (Adler, 1996: 85).

My own attempt to integrate my spiritual life into my work has been influenced in my early adulthood by various meditative and healing practices and, over the past twenty years or so, by Quakerism. Quakers (or more correctly, members of the Religious Society of Friends) believe that there is that of God (or the divine) in everyone. Hence, when I meet a client for the first time in movement, I attempt to let go of any preconceptions of who this is, and to contact what I see as the 'essence' of the human being, from my own essence. In this way, I can envisage us both linked into a 'higher source'. Either of us may derive some illumination or guidance from this higher source. The only difference is that my role as therapist is to channel that energy in the service of my client's decision to become more fully who she or he really is. From my discussions with psychodramatists, the kind of 'tuning in' to the client that I do is similar to their concept of 'tele' (see Wilkins, 1999 for a description of this phenomenon).

Whether this spiritual connection is 'real' or merely metaphoric is open to question, of course. However, by focussing on the idea I strengthen my intention, which is to respond to the client from outside of my own ego needs and to 'tune in' to the client's often unspoken, symbolic and metaphoric communication.

Summary and Conclusions

In this chapter I have deliberately limited my discussion of DMT theory to the concept of the movement metaphor within the creative process of change. In so doing, I have paid little attention to theories of verbal psychotherapy or of child development. I do not wish to imply, however, that these are irrelevant to DMT practice. They can be reviewed in any of the major texts on those subjects. My intention has been to focus on my central thesis, that DMT is a psychotherapy in its own right, mediated by the creative process within a therapeutic relationship, and using movement metaphor as its central tool. Having set this context for the work, it is now time to look at the journey into DMT praxis.

Notes

1 The term 'mother' is used here to denote the role of primary caregiver. This role is often, though not exclusively, taken by the biological mother and may be taken by a person of either sex. Additionally, other relationships within the family are likely to be significant within this role.

2 For a discussion of the system operating for maintenance of posture, see Meekums (1977).

PART II
The Journey

3

PREPARATION: WARMING UP AND GETTING STARTED

In this chapter I will be examining the beginnings of therapy in DMT. In Chapter 2 I showed how I conceptualise this in terms of the preparation phase of the creative process. I will present case material from my own clinical experience to illustrate the points I will be making. What I present in this and the next two chapters is my own approach, based on many years of clinical experience. It is not the last word on how to practise DMT, and is certainly not a substitute for formal training. My development so far has been based on dialectical growth borne out of clinical necessity. When I found that improvisation based on my training in release work (very similar to what is termed 'Authentic Movement') did not always work in adult psychiatry, I had to see what else within my repertoire might be of use. On the other hand, I found that improvisation based on internal imagery worked very well with some people, particularly those who were functioning reasonably well in terms of employment, relationships and so on (in psycho-dynamic terms, those with some 'ego strength'). I have developed my 'containment' approach to DMT, described below, in response to the needs of clients whose behaviour and/or cognitions indicate a risk to self and/or others. This category includes, but is not confined to, those individuals whose mental health symptoms are consistent with a borderline personality disorder diagnosis (American Psychiatric Association, 1994).

Formal Assessments

The decision about whether or not a formal assessment should take place on meeting a new client will depend on the context. Dance movement therapists work in a wide variety of settings. My own clinical experience has ranged from open groups in acute psychiatry, for example, to individual DMT as a primary psycho-therapeutic intervention.

I will illustrate this difference by describing a first session in an open ward group:

> *I do not know who is going to turn up this week. Bethany, whom I met last week, has gone shopping, accompanied by a member of the ward staff. Howard was admitted last night. Some of the staff have not yet got to know him, including the nurse assigned to hand over information to me. I quickly scan the risk assessment carried out by his community care co-ordinator, a copy of which is in his medical notes held on the ward. The assessment, and the fact that the staff do not deem it necessary to 'special' him (that is, use very frequent observations), is enough to convince me that he is not likely to be a danger to himself or others. I decide to invite him to my group, knowing that next week he may not be there. This may be his only chance to get whatever he can from what I have to offer. His involvement allows me to make observations that I hope can, through the few lines I will write in the multidisciplinary notes, contribute to the overall assessment being carried out during his in-patient stay.*

The above situation is in contrast to a DMT psychotherapeutic assessment:

> *Harriet and I have known for some time that we will meet. She was referred to me by her community care co-ordinator. The care co-ordinator felt DMT might be appropriate as Harriet's symptoms are largely focussed in her body. She suffers periods of depersonalisation, which she describes as feeling out of touch with her body, usually accompanied by a feeling of being somehow 'not here', an observer of all that happens to her. She has a mild eating disorder, and at times of stress she burns herself with cigarette butts, something she*

has been doing for years. She also binge drinks, resulting in risk to herself as she has on occasion slept rough when drunk.

I have sent her an appointment, and a map of how to get to me. The studio is small and inviting, with brightly coloured curtains and two easy chairs by a coffee table. There are a few art works on the walls, securely fastened. The secure fastening means that clients do not worry about aiming props, including a big soft ball, at the wall. There is a video camera fixed to one wall, and an overhead microphone. Harriet notices the equipment as soon as we are seated, and I explain that it is not turned on. I also explain that, from time to time, I do use this equipment in my work, but only if the person concerned feels OK about this and has signed to indicate their agreement. Refusal of the video does not affect anyone's right to treatment. I also reassure Harriet that I will not be asking her if I can video her today, but if she wants to know any more about how or why the video camera is used I will happily answer her questions.

I then explain: 'The purpose of our meeting today is for what we call an assessment interview. This is not a test and there are no right or wrong answers. The purpose is for you and I both to come to some sense of whether DMT might be of use to you, in your efforts to feel better about yourself and your life.' I explain that I usually meet people at least twice, unless it is clear to both of us from the outset that we are on the wrong track. I also tell her that when we have come to a formulation about how to proceed, I will draft a report for Harriet's care co-ordinator and meet with Harriet again, to read this to her before having it typed and sent. I tell her that my current practice is also to send a copy to the General (Medical) Practitioner, and to the Psychiatrist if there is one.

If I am meeting a client for the first time outside of the NHS, the list of people with whom I communicate may differ, depending on the setting. Sometimes I will write a re-formulation letter to the client, for her to keep. Such letters are deeply personalised, based on the model of cognitive analytic therapy (Ryle, 1997). A fictionalised reformulation letter is given in Figure 3.1.

Dear Harriet,

When you came to me to discuss the possibility of dance movement therapy you were concerned about feeling at times out of touch with your body. These periods of 'absence' were becoming quite distressing for you, as they were accompanied by feelings of unreality, as if you were an observer rather than really here. You also told me that you tend to alternately starve and binge, and have recently begun making yourself vomit after eating. This affords you a greater sense of control over your weight, although you had not considered the possible adverse effects on your health of this to do with nutritional deficiency, alterations in you blood electrolyte balance that might make you vulnerable to heart attacks, and damage to your oesophagus. For years you have tended to burn your skin at times of stress. You describe this as a way of staying alive. However, it does reinforce your view of yourself as worthless. This is something you want to change.

In order to understand some of these ways of coping, we looked at how life was for you as you were growing up. You described a fairly happy childhood up to the age of eleven years, when you were sent to boarding school. It was there that you were bullied and called 'fatso'. You discovered that you could go long periods without eating, and learned to hide food so that the staff thought you had had a good meal. This strategy worked reasonably well despite the trauma of the break-up of your parents' marriage, until you were raped by the father of one of your new school friends at the age of fourteen, during the summer break. The resulting pregnancy was discovered by one of the staff just before the Christmas vacation, and you were sent home in disgrace. You tried to keep the pregnancy and your suspension from school a secret from you parents because you believed the man who had raped you when he had said that it was your fault for wearing a short skirt. You tried to abort the foetus with hot baths and your mother's gin. You feigned illness for several weeks to delay going back to school, hoping that your period would magically start. Eventually, your mother realised that you were pregnant. When your step-father discovered this information he also raped you. You gave birth prematurely to a stillborn girl.

It was after this that your self-loathing really developed, and emotionally you hit rock bottom. You contemplated suicide, but instead began drinking secretly, and took up smoking. On one occasion, after anaesthetising yourself with drink, you stubbed out your cigarette on one of your arms. For a while it felt good, knowing that you had 'punished' yourself for what you saw as your own badness. The burn mark was more easily understandable than the emotional pain you felt inside. Harming yourself became a way of surviving. You started to wear long sleeves to cover up the marks, and began to sleep with boys not because you enjoyed it, but because you felt you were now 'used' and likely to be used again if you did not control it. You learned to cope by cutting off from your feelings and day-dreaming. This developed into the 'out of body' experiences you described to me when we met.

It seems to me that the fundamental problem you now face is that you have become alienated from you own body. You derive no pleasurable sensation from it. You are also endlessly critical of its appearance. Our aim in using dance movement therapy as your treatment will be to help you to tolerate some feeling and expression through your body. This will be an important beginning towards repairing some of the damage done by others to you over the years. We will also work on how the signals you send out through your non-verbal communication can be developed to best protect you. You will be absolutely in charge of how we go about this process. There will be times when you will find it scary to be in your body, due to its association with the past. You may even at times see me as one of the people that might hurt you. You might try to hurt my feelings in some way, albeit probably unconsciously. Or you may hope that I can be perfect in a way that the people who were meant to care for and protect you were not. I may become a disappointment to you when you see that I am only human. And it may become very difficult to face the ending of therapy.

Whatever we face in this journey of discovery, I have been struck by the strength with which you have survived all these years. I am sure that you can survive this. You deserve more than the 'existence' you have described to me. You deserve to live.

Yours sincerely,
Bonnie

Figure 3.1   *Harriet's Reformulation Letter*

What happens in the rest of the assessment time will depend on what information I have already, and on what the client needs to know. As a minimum, either in written information received at referral and/or during assessment appointments, I cover the following:

1 Information about DMT
I describe a typical DMT session. I explain that we always begin with a warm-up to mobilise and energise our bodies, and that after the warm-up we develop into more creative/symbolic work, arising from themes that emerge during the warm-up[1] or from the previous session. In the creative/symbolic part of the session[2] we often make use of a prop. Examples of props, which are easily visible to the client in the studio and can be pointed out to or handled by the client, include large physiotherapy balls, smaller football-sized foam balls, hoola hoops, stretch cloth and fans.

I explain to the client that after the creative section of the session, the ending of which is an organic development from the movement material, we usually sit together and discuss what has happened, including any symbolic content of the movement. Some of this may have been verbalised during the creative movement section of the session. However, our task at this stage in the session is not simply to raise awareness of the symbolic content of the movement but to examine how this insight can be used in everyday life, in particular in relation to the goals we have agreed at assessment.

At some stage during the assessment I invite the client to try a warm-up and some work with a prop. I emphasise that, whilst none of the movements I will suggest are likely to be injurious in themselves, it is important to pay attention to personal body cues. If any discomfort is experienced, it is best not to perform that particular movement. I also ask about any medical conditions. Since some clients will tend to ignore physical pain, I also monitor the client's movement, suggesting adjustments to avoid joint or muscle strain.

2 History

I ask for brief details regarding personal history, in narrative form. This will run rather like a conversation, in which I interject in the story from time to time to ask for clarification on some issue. I 'listen' not just to the 'facts' with my left brain, but to themes and metaphors, and to the client's non-verbal communication with my right brain. What emerges is a picture of how the client arrived at their current situation and what patterns the client may have brought with them from early attempts to cope with life experience. I take care to make sure that positive tales of relationships and bodily/movement experiences are elicited along with the inevitable tales of pain and suffering. My experience is that the therapy is much more likely to succeed if the client has had at least one positive relationship, and has at least some positive body memories. Positive relationships may have become idealised. For example, a dead grandmother may be conceptualised as a potential rescuer if only she had lived. When this happens I find that the client often either idealises me or expects to be hurt by me, rather than seeing me as a fallible human being who is nevertheless 'good enough'. This places the focus of the therapy squarely within the therapeutic movement relationship. On the other hand, the client may have learned that human beings are fallible. There may be sufficient experience of broadly positive relationships to know that we can together survive this fallibility. If so, I can be used as a witness and ally in addressing a different focus, for example learning to love one's body again (bearing in mind that most of us are delighted with our bodies when we first discover them as infants).

3 Risk Assessment

A mental health key worker/care co-ordinator may have carried out risk assessment prior to referring the client for DMT. er, if I have not seen a risk assessment, I will carry one out In any event, I will want to know how the therapy might ssues of risk. I am concerned here both with the client's al risk to self and any risk to others. Space does not allow here for a full breakdown of how to carry out a risk assessment. This requires specialist training. However, it is important to make the point that the meaning of the client's acts is more important than objective appraisal of those acts. For example, if the client spent some time feeling life is futile before deciding that suicide was the only option, then deliberated on how to carry out this decision, it doesn't matter that the overdose consisted of a relatively harmless herbal medicine. If the person thought the overdose would be fatal, then that was the intent. Such a client will try again unless something or someone intervenes to enable a different view of life. If, on the other hand, the person self-cuts as a way of deflecting away from emotional pain towards something more visible and understandable, this is far from a suicide attempt and is in fact a survival strategy (Spandler, 1996). I therefore ask all clients how they cope with stress, including what options they have open to them. I ask whether they can envisage therapy bringing up issues and feelings that they might find difficult. I tell all my clients that it is normal in therapy to feel worse before feeling better, often using the analogy of the influenza 'healing crisis' or of cleaning a deep wound. But, as with influenza or the wound, it is important not to rush back to your usual coping style without facing the crisis. If you do, things may get worse. I ask direct questions of clients about how they cope with anger, whether they direct this inwards in some way (and how/when), or take it out on others inappropriately (and how/when), or are able to assert themselves. I also ask directly whether they have ever done anything deliberately to themselves that might be harmful, like cutting or burning their skin, hitting themselves, eating or drinking harmful substances. If the answer is yes, I want to know under what circumstances, how frequently and how recently, so that I can begin to see if there is a pattern to this. I ask about drug use, both illegal and legal (including alcohol, coffee and tobacco). I am also interested in who my client can call on in times of distress and with whom they may be able to discuss the therapy. Will that person be supportive of the therapy, or undermining?

4 Movement Profiling
This is a particular skill of dance movement therapists and others trained in movement observation. I gave a brief outline of movement observation in Chapter 2. Figure 3.2 shows Harriet's (fictitious) movement profile.

Key: ✔ indicates presence of this attribute
Name of Client: *Harriet Smith*
Name of Profiler: *Bonnie Meekums*
Date of Profile: *1.1.2000*

Body Attitude
Sunken posture ✔
Over-erect, held posture
Naturally upright posture
Closed posture (where) ✔ *(leaning forward, arms crossed over stomach)*
Open posture (where)
Left/right split (list how they behave differently)
Upper/lower split (list how they behave differently) ✔ *(lower body held, even when upper body relatively fluid)*
Contralaterality in walk ✔ *(reduced)*
No contralaterality in walk
Bizarre or repeated movements ✔ *(right foot agitatedly flicking)*

Use of Space and Shaping
Small kinesphere (little use of personal space, making interaction with others difficult) ✔
Average kinesphere (making non-verbal interaction flow)
Extended kinesphere (potentially invasive of therapist's personal space)
Diffuse or unclear use of space
Linear use of space
Sculpting, moulded use of space

Efforts Used
Strong force (as in pushing, clapping)
Light force (as in delicate needlework, blowing bubbles)
Direct use space (as in eye contact, pointing)
Flexible use of space (as in looking around, describing an arc with hands)
Accelerating/Quickness (as in quick reactions)
Decelerating/Sustainment (taking one's time) ✔ *(slow to respond, hesitant)*
Bound flow (holding back, bodily tension, control over movements) ✔++
Free flow (going with the movement, a sense of abandonment)

Rhythms Used

Oral libidinal (rocking, stroking, sucking) ✔
Oral sadistic (biting, clenching and unclenching fists, picking at skin or nails, tapping foot or hand) ✔
Urethral libidinal (unable to stop, hardly pausing for breath)
Urethral sadistic (stop and go rhythms very apparent, as in verbal outpouring followed by silence)
Anal libidinal (twisting, wringing, e.g. of a piece of paper between fingers) ✔
Anal sadistic (holding on, e.g. to the breath, then letting go expulsively)

Phrasing

Impulsive (emphasis at the beginning of the phrase, e.g. suddenly getting out of the chair) ✔
Impactive (emphasis at the end of the phrase, e.g. fist to palm, to make a point)
Swing (e.g. 'on the one hand this, on the other hand that', with accompanying gesture)

Movement Metaphor

'I daren't reach out to others, because if I do I will not be in control and might get hurt, or hurt them.'

Formulation

Harriet's presentation may have been affected by the strangeness of the situation for her. Her small kinesphere, bound flow and closed posture indicate wariness. Her use of oral rhythms indicate the need for self-soothing, though any attempts may become destructive, given the use of sadistic rhythms. Her poor impulse control is evident in the use of impulsive phrasing. Her overall movement metaphor is noted above.
I would therefore focus the therapy on three goals:

1 *The development of a therapeutic alliance through shared movement, with respect for Harriet's tolerance levels for this and with her in control.*
2 *The development of impulse control through mastery of movement. An emphasis on different rhythmic structures including the urethral stop–go rhythm.*
3 *Exploration of relationship issues and themes of taking, holding and letting go/ending.*

Figure 3.2   *Harriet's Movement Profile*

The practice of movement observation used by dance movement therapists provides the clinically relevant possibility of a formulation-driven intervention, grounded in the movement metaphor. The movement profile is to the dance movement therapist what the written or diagrammatic formulation is to a cognitive-behavioural therapist, the reformulation is to a cognitive-analytical therapist, or the psychodynamic formulation is to the psychodynamic psychotherapist. That is, it provides an explanatory picture of the client's presentation and gives indications for 'treatment'. In so far as the movement profile gives information on both current attitudes, developmental stages, coping styles and patterns of relating, it most closely corresponds to the cognitive-analytic reformulation. Cognitive-behavioural formulations give less emphasis to the interactional aspects of the client's world and psychodynamic formulations stress intrapsychic phenomena more than behaviour. Whilst there are commonalities between the cognitive-analytic reformulation and the DMT formulation based on movement profiling, there are distinct differences. The DMT formulation as I use it is grounded in the movement metaphor. This gives both the dance movement therapist and the client insight into the central issues and themes in the client's life at the moment, the relevance of these for the therapeutic relationship, and how these insights might guide treatment using DMT as the treatment modality. The movement profile supports information obtained verbally, enabling client and therapist collaboratively to suggest one or two main foci for time-limited (20 to 24 session) DMT.

Short Term versus Long Term DMT

I do also work much longer term with clients, when the need arises, although much of my work currently in the British National Health Service (NHS) is geared towards time-limited, focused interventions. This development has occurred in response to strategic developments determined by a convergence of both financial and clinical concerns. The financial thrust is towards saving money and streamlining services to become more efficient. The clinical concern is one that I initially resisted. Working often with clients whose childhood had been deprived of love and affection, it was easy to assume that long-term therapy might offer the opportunity for 'reparenting'. My clients often took months to begin to trust me at all, so that deeper more insight-orientated work could not occur until after the period of time I currently offer. However, exposure to the work of Ryle (1990, 1997) and others has convinced me that there is a way to work quite briefly even with people who have suffered traumatic pasts. I have been forced to address that part of myself that would like to rescue others, and to examine the possibility that this might disable individuals in their quest to rescue themselves. I have been inspired by the writings of Sue Jennings (1996), an eminent dramatherapist, on this topic. I have also been struck by the very brief work offered by some counsellors that nevertheless has challenged the individual's 'conditions of worth' and thereby effected significant positive change.

Personal Safety

Personal safety for the therapist is important, particularly in any new encounter with a client. This is partly due to the aroused state in which some clients may arrive for their first session. Anxiety can lead to presuppositions, based on previous experience. For example, the client who has met hostile reactions from others in the past, for whatever reason, may be expecting similar behaviour from the therapist. This may lead to hypervigilence and a misreading of cues. One coping strategy might be to strike before the attack, be this verbally or physically.

It is common practice for therapists to position themselves for the first interview near to the door. If possible, another member of staff should be available for back-up, perhaps working in a nearby office. It is also important to adopt a non-confrontational body attitude. This means not leaning forward or back, sitting in a relaxed manner, taking care to keep all movements small and light, modulating voice tone and maintaining gentle eye contact. The therapist's eyes need to be relaxed to take in the whole picture of client movements. Above all, therapists need to learn to trust their impulses. Unless the therapist feels unsafe in all new situations (which presents a supervision, therapy and/or training issue), feeling unsafe should be treated seriously and therapists should feel justified in terminating prematurely any interview in which such feelings arise. For example, if the client moves suddenly out of the chair and towards the therapist, this may indicate impulsivity and aggression.

I should emphasise that these simple safety rules should not be interpreted as indicating that all therapeutic encounters are by their very nature dangerous. In all cases, it should be remembered that the therapist has the greater power and needs to work to put the client at ease.

A Safe Space

Personal safety of the client is also important. A hazard-free floor is a necessity. A sprung floor is ideal, though rare, and therapists must be constantly aware of the dangers of dancing on typical NHS floors, which tend to have a layer of concrete over floorboards, a practice which is potentially injurious to knees and other vulnerable joints. Jumping should be discouraged on these floors, sadly, as should stamping, although most ordinary sports shoes reduce the risk.

As important as the physical safety of the space is the need for privacy and confidentiality. The studio must not be overlooked, or must have adequate curtains or blinds. There must be a degree of soundproofing. And it is important that other staff understand the importance of not interrupting, as the following example shows.

It is the second session on the ward. We are in the middle of a process. I am holding Ivy's hands and we are dancing together. She is telling me how much she loves her family. Suddenly, a nurse enters the room, walks up to Ivy and suggests in a loud voice that Ivy should come for a walk. I resolve to put notices on the doors next week.

These situations are difficult, and it is important to view them from all perspectives. It is very likely that the nurse was a junior member of staff, carrying out orders that fitted in with the care plan for that individual. The group was new and so not all staff would have been fully aware of its existence, due to shift patterns, annual leave, sickness and so on. There is no reason why nurses should fully appreciate (in the early 1990s as this was) the need for privacy, given that they in all probability thought this was a dance class rather than a dance movement therapy session. They would not necessarily know the implications of the latter. Dance movement therapists can be seen as 'precious' or 'deliberately mysterious' in their insistence on covering up windows and doors and putting up 'do not disturb' notices (Meier, 1997). It does not help multidisciplinary working to be heavy handed about this. A mutual dialogue between professional groups can be fruitful, though, provided that each attempts to understand the professional constraints and ethics of the other. I have seen this kind of dialogue work well over a long period of time, resulting in more generally 'therapeutic' hospital environments, mutual respect and an increased sense of being valued on both sides.

Issues of Consent

I once had a particularly difficult situation when entering a ward day room to run a session. The ward was for people over the age of 65 with a range of mental health needs. I respectfully asked the clients if I could switch off the television. The response was: 'No you can't! Go and play somewhere else!' I was reminded of older people I knew in my neighbourhood when I was young, who always objected to me playing near their houses. For a split second, I was back there, no longer the therapist working respectfully with elders, but the stroppy eight-year-old kid who resented being told to go play somewhere else. Of course, this lasted a very short time and was not acted upon. I recovered my senses and was able to empathise with the desperate plight of someone who has precious little control over her environment. In the end, I was allowed to continue with the session and the lady in question looked on with curiosity, eventually joining in.

The issue of consent forms comes up frequently. It is good practice to ask for signed consent before using case material for a book such as this, for example, and signed consent for the use of video recordings for supervision or training purposes. However, for one frail older woman, this respectful gesture presented her with a dilemma. She was convinced, despite my attempts to explain the purpose to her, that she was 'signing herself in' to hospital, and thus her liberty away. In such circumstances it may be wiser to ask someone to act as advocate. However, this practice demands staff, family or volunteer time that may not always be available.

When contact with a client is brief, for example for one session as in an open ward group, paperwork becomes cumbersome and can exceed time spent in therapeutic contact. I have not found an entirely satisfactory solution to the problem of consent to the use of case material in such situations. My best attempt so far is to disguise the narrative in some way, and make use of composite cases.

The Therapeutic Relationship

DMT occurs within a therapeutic relationship. The conditions identified by Rogers (1957) are an important aspect of that relationship. Thus, the therapist strives towards unconditional positive regard for all clients, aims to convey genuine warmth, and makes use of the self within a real human relationship. Wilkins (2000) argues that the counsellor or therapist's ability to communicate unconditional positive regard to the client is the most crucial therapeutic factor, regardless of discipline. Being influenced by the humanistic paradigm, I aim to be as 'real' with my clients as possible, without forgetting what I am there for. Thus, it might be appropriate at times to say that I have children and can empathise with a mother's frustrations in trying to balance her own needs and the needs of her children. On other occasions, it might be important to wait before giving this information. At all times, I must avoid slipping into 'chatting' about my offspring, even if the client tries to get me to do so! This would turn the relationship into something other than a professional helping relationship. But if what a client is saying or doing moves me, I allow that to show. The boundary is drawn in that I would never sob uncontrollably, look shocked, or express the client's anger for them. In short, my expressed affect as the therapist is always at least one notch down from that potentially expressed or contained by the client, and remains contained.

Dance movement therapists pay special attention to the non-verbal aspects of the therapeutic relationship. I should emphasise here that this does not mean that every postural shift is conscious. I often 'come to' during a piece of verbal interaction, to realise that I have adopted a mirrored stance or shifted my position and breathed a sigh at the same time roughly as the client. It is difficult to contrive this level of empathy.

However, there is a conscious aspect to empathic reflection during the DMT process. Much of our awareness of this has come from the work of Marian Chace, who described empathic movement reflection in DMT or 'mirroring' (Levy, 1992). In this technique, the therapist moves with the client and reflects something of the quality of the movement, not necessarily reproducing every aspect. The aspects that are reflected are often intuitively chosen, but may be particularly significant for the person concerned. This aspect can then be amplified or modified in some way, perhaps to illustrate new possibilities. It is worth quoting from Levy (1992: 25–6) to illustrate this process:

> By taking the patient's nonverbal and symbolic communications seriously, and helping to broaden, expand and clarify them, Chace demonstrated her immediate desire and ability to meet the patient 'where

he/she is' emotionally and thus to understand and accept the patient on a deep and genuine level. In essence, Chace said to her patients, in movement, 'I understand you, I hear you and it's okay.' In this sense she helped to validate the patient's immediate experience of him/herself.

An example from my own clinical work illustrates Levy's point. The vignette also highlights the role of seeing and being seen, which I feel constitutes the physical origin and thus metaphor for psychological insight. Mutual gaze, and the infant's experience of the mother's smile, are important aspects of early mirroring for the sighted infant, and thus of positive self-evaluation and later affect regulation (Schore, 1994, 2001).

John's parents had favoured his older brother. Whenever John achieved anything, his achievements were ignored or minimised, leaving him with a strong sense that he would never be good enough. He developed an obsessive habit of checking his appearance in mirrors. He also adopted a rather haughty attitude to others, characterised by a particular movement in which he would pull his chin back (distancing himself) and up (elevating himself), fixing his gaze and pursing his lips. His vocalisations would adopt a sarcastic, abrasive character both in tone and content at this stage. He remained unaware of his effect on others and was hurt by their reactions to him.

I concluded that John's difficulties were associated with narcissistic pain. His sense of worthlessness was defended against by his attempts to distance and elevate himself in relation to others, but in fact this resulted in envious attack and thus maintained his problem.

I decided to work on mirroring his movements, as recommended by Lewis Bernstein (1986) for people with narcissistic traits. I noticed that when he began to lead the movement, he immediately turned his back on me. I was left with the option of turning my back also (and not seeing him), shadowing him from behind, or moving alongside him. I could not face him, as he was too near the wall, and besides I felt this would be too confronting. I chose to move alongside him.

When we stopped moving, I fed back my observations and suggested we repeat the exercise, but that he 'keep me in view' and see if he could 'take me in'. Seconds after we began again to move together, he stopped. Tears welled up in his eyes. I asked him what he was feeling, and he reflected: 'No-one has ever been with me before. I've always been alone.'

Checking In

I usually begin each session with some kind of check-in. This allows group members to share something of how they are feeling and any important news. In some groups, the check-in will be verbal, but in others it is purely non-verbal. A simple form of check-in is for group members in turn to make a movement for how they feel today. The group typically mirrors each person's contribution back to the individual as a way of expressing empathy.

The Warm-up

In the warm-up, I will take the group through some or all of the following elements, accompanied by some music:

● Stretching in various directions to begin to relate to the space around and connect the extremities to the centre of our bodies.

● Shaking of body parts to aid relaxation and awaken awareness of our bodies as a whole and gentle rubbing or patting of our bodies to increase awareness of body boundaries, that is, where we begin and end.

● Foot exercises to deepen contact with the ground and improve stability.

● Gentle spinal twists, bends and stretches to increase a sense of alignment and connectedness through the centre of our bodies.

● Movements co-ordinated with the breath to deepen awareness of our breathing and bring it into efficient harmony with action.

● Gentle tension followed by release to work on relaxation and energising and to improve circulation.

● Arm swings to develop a sense of flow and ease in our movement.

● The beginnings of symbolic movement, for example reaching into space as if reaching for something, or shaking our hands as if shaking something off.

Towards the end of the warm-up, we may work together on one body part that has emerged as significant for the client or that the client feels has been ignored and still needs some work.

Containment

The early stages of any therapy will tend to focus on setting the conditions of safety that will allow clients later to explore whatever it is that they need to explore. One of these safety conditions is often referred to as 'containment'. I do not use this word to mean restraint of the client. In some settings, physical restraint may be used, for example if a client becomes physically aggressive. However, the need for this is rare provided that the therapist pays attention to personal safety (see above).

The containment to which I refer here has a more psychodynamic, metaphoric significance. It has to do with the client's need that material raised through DMT will not be overwhelming. The idea is to promote an internal locus of control, that is, for clients to feel able to control their own impulses and responses. There is also a sense in which one is working towards a cohesive, boundaried and contained sense of self as opposed to the fragmentation experienced by some people with mental health needs.

For people labelled as suffering from a borderline personality disorder (BPD), impulsive behaviour including self-injury may be the norm. Mental Health Services sometimes respond by using external controls that might be perceived as invasive, judgmental and punitive. Many of those presenting with the symptom picture associated with BPD have suffered childhood abuse (Beitchman et al., 1992; Green, 1993). This kind of service response replicates that abusive experience and further disempowers the individual. Many services are beginning to realise this dilemma and are responding by raising staff awareness. In some areas, new services are being developed, designed to help clients to cope with their intrusive thoughts and dissociative states. Dissociative states are characterised by a sense of alienation from the body accompanied by a sense of unreality and/or 'flashbacks' in which past trauma is relived as if it were happening in the present.

The containment approach to DMT that I am proposing here would fit in with this new thrust in service provision. The goals of this approach are summarised in Figure 3.3.

✔ To reinforce the individual's right to engage or disengage with what is on offer during the session.
✔ To enable clients to feel more in control of their own impulses.
✔ To increase bodily and sensory awareness, as a counter thrust to depersonalisation (alienation from the body).
✔ To emphasise body/self boundaries.
✔ To increase a sense of control over body boundaries.
✔ In group DMT, to reinforce the sense of the group as a whole, in its containing and supportive function.
✔ To limit the impact of emotionally charged issues.
✔ To increase positive bodily experiences.

Figure 3.3   *Aims of the Containment Approach to DMT*

Some of the techniques I use in order to work towards containment are summarised in Figure 3.4. They are:

✔ The negotiation of group agreements
✔ Keeping strict time boundaries
✔ The right to say no
✔ The use of rhythmic structure
✔ Working with stop and go
✔ Working with props projectively
✔ Body boundaries
✔ Breathing techniques
✔ Grounding techniques
✔ Exploration of personal space
✔ Redirecting energy
✔ Symbolic work: taking, holding and letting go
✔ Shared movement (circular formation)
✔ Finding an ending to the improvisation
✔ Choreography

Figure 3.4   *Strategies for Containment in DMT*

1 The Negotiation of Group Agreements
These can provide real security for group participants. For example:

Angela was very concerned when she arrived at her first DMT session and discovered that a neighbour of hers was also in the group. They lived in a tight-knit community in which everyone knew everyone else's business. She was greatly reassured when I suggested that the content of the sessions should be confidential. We spent some time defining precisely what we meant by this. From my previous clinical experience, I knew that it was wise to ask that issues about group interaction, whether or not these arose within the session, should be brought to the session rather than discussed elsewhere. I also said that the membership list of the group was confidential. Group members could speak of their own experience to loved ones but could not identify anyone else in their discussions. I explained the limits to confidentiality. I said that I would receive clinical supervision to aid me in my thinking about the group but would only use first names; and that I would share important information with the team caring for each individual on a 'need to know' basis. If I was concerned about anybody, including a vulnerable person not in the group, I would first of all raise the issue with the group and help them to decide how to act. However, there were some legal constraints on me. For example, an individual might disclose that the person who sexually abused them years ago is now living with a woman who has small children. I explained that if any group member disclosing such information is unwilling or unable to act, I have to ring the child protection team of the local social services department. In so doing, I make every effort to protect the confidentiality of my informant.

2 Keeping Strict Time Boundaries

Sessions normally start and finish on time. This can be very difficult for therapists to enforce. There may be people who feel that it is unfair to finish the session. However, the acceptance of boundaries can be a very important development. Boundaries are there to provide a benevolent container. Time boundaries mean that the client only has to face certain difficult material for that given time each week. They also encourage people to take responsibility for dealing with issues in a timely manner, rather than waiting and hoping that someone will take the initiative for them. They encourage the group to negotiate turn taking. Above all, they mean that clients are encouraged to deal with their issues around endings, whatever they may be.

It is usual in my DMT groups to make use of a closing ritual, to allow group members to identify and cope with the end of the session. Ritual seems to have a deep social and psychological significance in enabling groups and individuals to process transitions. Hence, we have rituals associated even in the West with birth, death, marriage, anniversaries and puberty. Countless more idiosyncratic rituals are performed for going to bed, waking up, coming home from work and so on. They bring a sense of familiarity and control into what otherwise might remind us of times when we felt powerless in the face of loss. The familiarity and benevolent connection to others in shared rituals can help us to cope and enable us to adopt a more accepting frame of mind.

I often use structures within a circle at the beginning and end of the group, because the circle both reaffirms group identity and provides a spatial metaphor of containment. Structures include either a verbal check-in seated on chairs or a movement check-in standing in the circle. The verbal check-in may be either unstructured, in which each group member says whatever they need to say, or it may be structured in some way. For example, each group member might be asked to describe how they feel in terms of weather. I might, for example, say that I am the lull before the storm, or a misty day on a cliff path. A movement check-in might allow for each person to introduce themselves as they are today, in terms of movement that is acknowledged and mirrored by the group as a whole.

The ending of the session might be a movement and breathing exercise, perhaps taken from martial arts or yoga, or it might be a grounding exercise (see below) or a simple circle dance performed to music. The circle dance might be taught to the group in the early sessions, or it might arise out of a group improvisation, emerging as the group's own choreographed dance. Such dances can be given names by the group. They are best derived from an improvisation on a very positive theme, for example 'power', 'protection' or 'connectedness'. I give a clinical example relating to the use of circle dance below, in the section on 'choreography'.

3 *The Right to Say No*
It is very important that clients are neither cajoled into participating, nor made to feel guilty if they do not wish to participate. If the assessment has been thorough, most clients have some sense of what DMT is and whether or not they are willing to participate. However, they may need to be told quite frequently in the early days that they have the right to opt out. One way to opt out is to stay in the circle, to mirror the movements of others along with the rest of the group but to choose not to contribute a movement in shared leadership. If regular reviews are held with individuals, the significance of this decision can be explored. Alternatively, the

therapist may wish to comment lightly during group discussion towards the end of the session, perhaps empathically reflecting how difficult it is to share something of oneself in a group and giving some helpful suggestions about where to start. One such suggestion is to choose a movement that has already been used, acknowledging that each person's version of this will be unique.

4 The Use of Rhythmic Structure

Rhythm has an organising function for us. A simple march is conducted in 2/4 time. The beat has a unifying, containing quality that encourages a discipline of the emotions. This is essential in training troops to follow orders and keep their impulses in check. A waltz, however, in 3/4 time, allows for greater freedom without complete loss of control. Thus the waltz became at a certain point in our history the dance of romantics.

The foetal heart rhythm is the one we most often use when soothing a baby. Later, we use a rhythm similar to the one used by nursing babies, when we sing lullabies and rock our little ones to sleep. For those adults who have not internalised these rhythms due to poor parenting experiences, it is hard to find the appropriate rhythm with their own children. There is a tendency to accelerate. Acceleration will be stimulating for an infant, rather than soothing. Music, however, helps us to keep an even beat. The music can be either pre-recorded or created through song.

When I have worked with groups of mothers and their young children, one of the children's favourite games has been 'blankets'.

> *I had a blanket in the studio. I suggested that each child could take turns to lie in the middle. Once Emily was in place, I encouraged Cassie, her mother, to position herself for eye contact. The whole group then stood evenly distributed around the blanket. We lifted the blanket, rocking it gently from side to side, and sang a lullaby. Mother and child looked at each other adoringly, supported in their interaction by the group as a whole.*

Another favourite is also mediated through song. I ask each mother to sit and cradle her toddler like a baby. It is important that the mother is sitting comfortably, perhaps with her back supported. The pair are then be able to make relaxed eye contact, as they sing and rock together. The words of the song are taken from a Sufi chant:

I love you, whether I know it or not
I love you, whether I show it or not
There are so many things I haven't
said inside my heart
And now is a good time to start

5 *Working with Stop and Go*

Working with stop and go is another way in which we can organise our movement temporally. One of our earliest experiences of containment is when we learn to control our bladders. The rhythmic structure through which we play with stopping and going as children mirrors this process. Small children love to run freely into a parent's arms and be stopped by the force of a familiar body. The action allows for the experience of free flow to be continued with a swing around, before placing the child carefully and unharmed on the ground. My own small son loves to 'race' me up the stairs to the bathroom, as part of his pre-bedtime ritual. Not only does he run with gusto and then stop at the top of the stairs, he also stops on occasion on the way up, spreading his little body wide to prevent me from overtaking him. He always wins.

For those children who do not have such containing relationships with adults, it may be difficult to internalise benevolent controls. This may be especially difficult if control and restraint have been exerted on the child in a solely punitive manner, as in the experience of physical or sexual abuse. I have known clients who imagined that if they allowed their tears to flow, they would never stop. Their solution was never to allow them to flow. Such clients may have difficulty in allowing the experience of free flow. They may also have difficulties in coping with clear endings (like the end of the session). Working with stop and go as an embodied phenomenon might be one way to address some of these issues.

One group of women, all of whom had histories of poor impulse control, were invited to attend the movement therapy group. I suggested that they move across a diagonal in the studio, first to a beat provided by me on a hand drum, then to a beat provided by each of them in turn. When the drum stopped, the group stopped moving. The women had varied speeds to their beat, and varied responses to it. I then suggested they try moving and stopping together without the drum, sensing their timing from each other. Some of them were wildly out of time with the others, but slowly over a number of weeks they came to enjoy this task, as it provided a challenge that was new to them but which they could master.

6 Working with Props Projectively

I have briefly listed above some of the props I use. Every dance movement therapist should have certain equipment, including a decent stereo and a range of music and props at their disposal.

The following props, summarised in Figure 3.5, are often used in DMT practice:

- Body bands (different colours)
- Stretch cloths, various colours, 1.5 metres by 1 metre
- Smaller circles or squares of stretch cloth
- Large physiotherapy balls
- Soft foam footballs
- Smaller sensory balls
- Range of percussion instruments
- Garden canes
- Soft toys
- Parachute
- Fans
- Small objects
- Drawings (including client's own)
- Stories (including client's own)
- Photographs
- Client's own objects

Figure 3.5 *Props for Projective DMT Work*

(a) A 'body band', which can be bought expensively from specialist suppliers but is just as good if home-made from a knotted piece of the widest elastic you can buy at your local market. I find it useful to have different colours of body band, since clients project personal meanings into the colour. The knot can also be a source of projection.

> *In one session, the women were passing the knot around the circle very quickly, as if it were something to be got rid of, reminding them of 'knotty' problems*

in their lives. But Eva said she wanted the knot; it reminded her of something quite different, and positive. The elastic itself became the umbilicus, binding the group together.

(b) More than one piece of stretch cloth, preferably large pieces, again in a variety of colours. It is good to include blue in this, as it can be used to make environments, becoming a river or other water source. Stretch cloths can be held by the group and provide a focus for movement which can include quite undulating ('oral') movement and more aggressive pulling actions. A soft ball can also be bounced on the top if the group chooses.

(c) Balls. These should be in various sizes, but all soft. Physiotherapists' catalogues and children's toy catalogues are the usual sources. A large physiotherapy ball can provide something to hold on to and squeeze, or to lie on top of and relax. A foam football can be used to throw and kick, with minimal risk of breakages and injury, whilst a small rubber ball can be squeezed and pounded.

(d) Other useful additions might include: a range of percussion instruments; fans for paired mirroring work; smaller circles or squares of stretch cloth for two people to hold onto and move with; garden canes for two people to hold, one between each pair of opposite hands making tramlines so that the pair can move together maintaining an even distance; soft toys, for clients to hold or project onto; a parachute; and whatever small objects might be useful for projective work.

I remember one training group in which a prop became particularly significant as a bridge for relating to others:

A young man called Graham attended. He was very open and enthusiastic, and wanted to learn new skills for his work in a family centre. I set up a paired exercise, in which each of the pair took turns to lead movement, the other mirroring. Each of them held a fan in one hand. After a while, I suggested that they experiment with no one leading, eventually finding the ending to their dance together, without discussing it. Afterwards, Graham commented that he had not felt so deeply at one with another human being in his adult life.

Another example comes to mind, from my individual clinical work:

> *Joanne and I moved together one day with the stretch cloth. I felt she was trying to pull me towards her, so I responded by pulling on my end of the cloth, to give her something to work against. She seemed to hesitate, the strength going out of her movement. I reflected verbally what I had seen; that first she pulled, then when I pulled too she went limp. Tears welled up in her eyes. I asked her what this reminded her of, and she told me that she dared not pull anyone close to her, for fear that they might die like her brother.*

7 Body Boundaries

Affirmation of body boundaries is very important for all of us. We live in a world of alienation from our bodies, with cars to get us from A to B and televisions or video games replacing sport as pastimes. When we do engage in activity, it is often in a punishing 'exercise programme'. For people suffering from psychotic or dissociative states, reconnection with the body self is of vital mental health importance. The boundaries of my body are where I end and you/the rest of the world begins. I need to know that.

I emphasise body boundaries in a variety of ways. Some of them were described above, in the section on warm-up. They include: patting and rubbing the skin; feeling contact with the floor, clothing and air during movement and stillness; and drawing round body parts (solo) or whole bodies (working with same-sex pairs within a group).

8 Breathing Techniques

Breathing is a constant reminder that we have an inside and an outside. Our bodies are containers. We can choose how we take in the air, how we receive it, how we expel it. Sometimes I suggest simply paying attention to the breath. However, this is not useful with clients who have a tendency towards anxiety, as attention to the breath will in some cases increase irregularities in breathing. I therefore use an integrative breathing and movement approach.

A simple exercise involves raising my hands up in front of my body along the mid-line, breathing in as I do so, to the point of a stretch above my head. I allow my gaze to follow my hands. I then open my hands away from each other, allowing them to describe an arc that continues all the way down to the floor as I breathe out. My knees bend as necessary to accommodate this action. I then gather my hands together, as if scooping something off the floor, bring my cupped palms up to chest level breathing in and straightening my legs, then turn my palms downwards and breathe out, returning my hands to my sides. I repeat the whole sequence as many times as seems useful.

Breathing is linked to the Flow Effort. The above exercise encourages smooth transitions between Bound and Free Flow, without over-emphasising Bound Flow as in the holding of breath or in laboured breathing. When we feel out of control we often try to exert control by holding our breath or by breathing very shallowly. Awareness of Flow is also important in controlling impulsivity and in maintaining energy levels. One way to increase awareness of Flow in the musculature is to use a simple tension-release exercise, linking this with the breath. I suggest that group members either lie down or sit in chairs, and close their eyes if this is comfortable or focus on a spot on the floor. Then I conduct a tour through the body, starting at the top and working downwards, tensing on the in breath and releasing on the out breath. In this way, the individual learns to modulate tension levels in the body and eventually relaxation can be performed in an instant.

9 Grounding Techniques

Grounding is one of those words that probably means different things to different people. I first came across the word through my contact with the 'growth movement' in London in the 1970s. For me, it refers both to my ability to perceive and live in the here and now, and to my contact with the ground. The first I do through my senses and my visceral awareness, including breathing techniques as described above. The second I do through various specific movement exercises.

Focusing on the senses is a very useful way to bring people back into their bodies when they are suffering from depersonalised states. For example, I suggest looking around and taking in what you see. I may suggest concentrating on the sounds outside, then inside the room, and provided that this would not be too distressing I may then suggest concentrating on the sounds inside one's body. For some groups, it is possible to set up a paired exercise in which one person closes his or her eyes, the other gently leading them around the room to touch, smell or feel whatever is available.

Windows can be opened and the sudden rush of air felt, pepper-mint tea can be smelled, a cloth can be gently draped over an arm and so on.

Specific movement exercises can include:

- Walk on different surfaces of the feet, or with awareness of the foot's anatomy. There are 26 bones in each foot, allowing for great flexibility, and the arch of the foot is constructed like an excellent piece of engineering, as a bridge that receives and distributes weight over the whole foot.

- Imagine walking on different surfaces, including soft sand in which an imprint can be made, or by contrast hot hard sand over which you run with very little contact. This allows for greater awareness of how you normally use your feet, whether you hardly touch the ground or give right into it, for example.

- Self-massage your feet. This can be done sitting down. One group participant with whom I did this remarked that she had completely forgotten about her feet and that it was nice to rediscover them in this way.

- Move across the floor by sliding your feet, as if skating.

- Pliés. Bend at the knees by allowing them to soften and move forwards over your toes, then straighten them by pushing into the ground.

- A stationary exercise, in which you move one foot at time, changing the surface that is in contact with the floor from whole foot through to the ball, to tips of the toes and off. To do this, you may need to have something nearby you can hold onto.

- Lunges, in which the previous exercise is used as one foot is placed down at some distance from the other, weight trans-ferred to that leg, then push down into the floor and rebound so that the foot leaves the floor, weight being transferred to the other leg.

- Jumps and skips, in which a similar action is used but allowing for the whole body to leave the floor. The emphasis here is not so much on leaving the floor but on pressing into the floor as preparation, then springing off from this position, making use of the momentum.

- In pairs, lean towards each other, making contact through the palms of your hands. It is useful if the two people in any one pair are roughly the same size and weight, though height is more important than weight. The task is to find a point of balance and to concentrate on the idea that some weight is transferred through the hands, the rest being transmitted down into the floor. The spine is one long line. Then, gradually begin to move together on the spot, forwards and backwards. Feet remain in one place and the spine remains in one long line. This exercise works on connectedness throughout the body, on relationship and on grounding all at the same time.

● Lean onto a physiotherapy ball.

> *Suzanne and I had been working together for a while. As a child, she had felt rejected, ignored or criticised by her parents. She had developed a dislike for her legs and constantly criticised them for not being the way she felt they should be. She ignored the sensations in her legs and so frequently bruised them. They were chronically tense and in pain, as if on guard for what might happen next. I became aware that she was treating her legs the way that she had been treated as a child, and that they were feeling the way she was feeling: unloved, ignored, in pain, bruised, criticised and never good enough. She chose a physiotherapy ball to move with and began to experiment with giving it her weight. But her disconnection from her legs meant that she held them tense and lost her connection also with her source of support, the ground. When she gave the ball her weight, she fell off. I suggested she relax her legs and allow her weight to sink downwards. She did so and found she was able to mould also into the ball with greater stability. She was then able to take in the nurturing aspects of her personal symbolism, as the ball reminded her of her grandmother's large, warm, soft breasts.*

● A style of walking I use, adapted from both Tai Chi Chuan and release work. In this exercise, I give a series of instructions similar to the following:

> *Stand first on your two legs, with the weight evenly distributed. Imagine that there is water inside your legs and that currently both legs are 'half full'. Your knees are gently relaxed, not 'locked back'. Now begin to transfer weight from one leg slowly to the other. As you do so,*

imagine that you are pouring water from the leg that is losing weight into the other, through a point in your pelvis just below the navel. This is your centre of gravity. Eventually, all of the weight is in one leg and this becomes 'full'. It is now possible to peel the foot belonging to the empty leg off the floor, letting it hang relaxed in the air. As you peel your foot off the floor, continue to balance around a strong centre of gravity. Allow weight to fall down to this point through a central line of gravity passing from the crown of your head through the centre of your torso and into your pelvis. Now place the relaxed foot down in a different spot and begin the process of weight transfer to that foot. Repeat the process so that your walk becomes like a movement meditation, an exercise in awareness as well as grounding.

- I also make use of visual imagery to develop grounding in stillness. Sometimes I do this to mark the ending of the session. We all stand in a circle, but not too close, and adopt a relaxed, aligned stance. Then I give instructions as follows:

Feel the weight on your feet, and play with where this falls by swaying a little from side to side and front to back. Now find a place where the weight falls evenly across both feet. Now notice your knees. If they are locked back, see if you can release them so that they are simply aligned, ready to allow you to move whenever you wish. Imagine a line through the centre of your body, beginning at the crown of your head and falling like a plumb line through your torso. This is your centre line of gravity and approximates to the spine. When the forces of gravity falling through your spine with all its curves are analysed, they end up as this perfectly straight line (Todd, 1937). Let your body rest around this central line of support. There is a law of physics that says that for every action there is an equal and opposite reaction. So as the force of your weight falls into the earth, the earth responds by giving you just the right amount of support. You can visualise this support as synchronised with your breath. On each in breath, allow the force from the earth to rise through your feet and legs, and to collect as a ball of energy at a point just below your navel. This is your centre of gravity, known in Japanese martial arts as the Hara. Now on the out breath, send this energy throughout your body – up through your centre line, out into your hands and down through your legs into the earth. You can extend this flow of energy out through your skin, to form your personal space. Maybe the energy has a particular colour, which will be different for everyone. What colour is your energy? Do you want to send it to one place in particular in your body that needs some support right now? Remember that the energy is limitless. There is always more to be had on each in-breath. Now try sending this energy around the group as an affirmation of our connectedness with each other. Our breath also connects at the centre of the earth, with all humanity.

Grounding techniques used in DMT are summarised in Figure 3.6.

- Walking on different surfaces of the foot
- Walking on different imagined surfaces
- Self-massage of feet
- Sliding across the floor
- Pliés
- Exercise: working through the foot
- Lunges
- Jumps and skips
- Leaning into a partner
- Leaning on a physiotherapy ball
- Tai Chi walk
- Guided visualisation

Figure 3.6   *Grounding Techniques in DMT*

10 Exploration of Personal Space

The personal space around our bodies can be considered to be an extension of our self-identity insofar as, when that notional space is encroached on by uninvited others, we can feel personally invaded. Of course, the statement that we do or do not invite others 'in' is not necessarily verbally mediated, nor is it always clear to those around us. But how we take up our personal space can often be an indicator of our willingness or otherwise to engage. An awareness of these issues is important, for example in assertiveness training.

In DMT, the personal space is usually referred to as the kinesphere, in acknowledgement that it is what you do with that personal space, how you move and are still within it, that is important in what is both felt and communicated. The kinesphere roughly equates to the reach space used by the individual. We will all know people who, when they walk into a room, seem to take up huge amounts of space. Such people may appear flamboyant, charismatic or aggressive. They have a large kinesphere. On the other end of the scale are those people who seem very unassuming, who perhaps go unnoticed or seem nervous and timid. In their presence we might be tempted either to try to 'draw them out of themselves' (an interesting metaphor that illustrates the kinesphere as an extension of the self) or feel that they are too much like hard work to bother with. We might even feel irritated with them, feeling they are rude and stand-offish. These individuals have a small kinesphere. In the middle are the people with whom we can easily engage, whom we feel we can trust and who trust us. There is a mutual give-and-take feel to the relationship. They (and we in that context) have average kinespheres. Of course, we all tend to move in and out of the three categories in different situations or frames of mind, and with different people. Provided we can do that, there is no problem. But some people do not have access to such flexibility. Those people can potentially benefit from exploring their kinespheres.

I encourage clients to explore their kinespheres in a number of ways. First, reaching exercises work on expanding kinaesthetic awareness. A second way to work on the issue is to set up a partner exercise. I will illustrate this with a clinical vignette.

Christine and Beryl were in the same therapy group. I decided to set up pair dances to develop the relationships within the group and to enable some discussion about relationships in general. I started off with an exercise in which the two people in any pair stood facing each other, holding two garden canes between their index fingertips like a bridge between them. I played some gentle music, and after modelling the exercise with my co-worker I suggested that the pair begin to move together, in whatever way they wished, but maintaining contact with the canes through their finger-tips. Christine and Beryl each worked with a different partner. In the verbal processing that followed, Christine said that she

*found the exercise too confronting and not at all relaxing,
whereas Beryl went on to develop her partner dance into
hand-to-hand contact, with which she felt perfectly comfortable and which she found very relaxing.*

The above clinical vignette illustrates the difficulties in setting up
some movement exercises in any group situation, due to the vast
variation in response. The important factor here was Christine's
right to choose the level of her involvement. For some clients,
garden canes provide a safe distance that cannot be breached,
enabling the individual to experiment with relating without fear of
invasion.

A third way to explore the kinesphere is to suggest that each
person imagines themselves inside a bubble, out of which they can
step at any time (this part of the instruction is very important, to
avoid claustrophobic associations). Moving to some soft and gentle
music, each person explores the edges of their bubble, as a three
dimensional structure. They can also play with changing its con-
sistency, shape and size, opening and closing it and so on.

I have worked with some people in pairs in a very simple
structure designed to increase control over personal space. One of
the pair moves slowly towards the other. At the point at which the
stationary partner begins to feel uncomfortable, they reach out in
front, as if to stop traffic with palm presenting, and say a firm
STOP! The mover stops. Roles are then reversed. To vary the
exercise, I sometimes suggest that the pairs play with speed,
direction, level (for example, crawling or creeping as opposed to
walking), imagined gender or identity, and so on.

In one women's group, I made use of the group as a whole to
assist the development of control over the kinesphere:

*Sheila was troubled by the voice she heard of a man who had
abused her in the past. At my suggestion, the whole group
assembled in a circle and made a karate-style punch and kick
into the centre of the circle. At the same time, we all shouted
'Leave us alone!' The atmosphere was electric, an affirmation
of every woman's (and man's and child's) right to live free
from personal invasion. The voice disappeared.*

11 Redirecting Energy

Occasionally, the kind of movements described above, like punch-
ing and kicking at the air, may arise spontaneously. A skilled

therapist, knowing the client, will be able to assess the risk of the movement becoming directed at another person or property. If such risk exists, it is possible to support the expression of aggression whilst making the situation safe by redirecting, structuring and possibly reducing the energy. One simple way to do this is to encourage a downward movement, at the same time rhythmically structuring it with the aid of music. Reduction of the energy can also be aided by music, if it changes quality to become more lyrical, before clearly coming to an end.

Props can provide a further way of redirecting energy because the focus is on the prop rather than on the body, thus providing some projective distance. The following vignette illustrates the usefulness of a prop in assisting one woman to safely express her anger:

Petra was very frightened that if she let out her anger it would take her out of control. I knew her sufficiently well to sense that this was not the case and predicted to her that she would become tired before that happened. I made use of a stretch cloth to give her something to hold on to; she pulled and tugged angrily at it, from time to time verbalising her thoughts. I held on to the other end, responding to her movement with my own. Eventually she said she was getting tired, but I had the sense that she had not finished and so I encouraged her to keep going. When I sensed that she had completed a process (shown in a clear change in her movement quality rather than an abrupt stop), I suggested that she find an ending. Afterwards, I asked her what she had learned from the process. She replied that she realised that her anger was not so overwhelming as she had imagined. Subsequent to that session, she reported feeling much calmer and less angry, which she attributed to a cognitive shift arising from the work.

Whilst there was undoubtedly catharsis in the session described above, the real shift came from the meaning Petra elicited from this experience rather than the transitory effects of energy release.

12 Symbolic Work: Taking and Holding and Letting Go
Most of us have issues to do with relationships. These can often be characterised in terms of attachment and loss. Clients who have

felt abandoned, for example, may stop reaching out to people ('reaching out' to someone is an example of a commonly-used movement metaphor). I am indebted to Shirley Summers, a gestalt therapist with a movement background, for a workshop I attended some years ago led by her on this movement theme. I have since used the ideas clinically with several of my clients. As a piece of symbolic work, the theme of taking, holding and letting go might fit best in the middle phase of therapy, which can be more exploratory. However, in this early phase it is possible to gently raise the client's awareness without necessarily deepening the exploration. Some examples were given above in the warm-up section. As a gentle introduction to symbolic work around this theme, I pose a question or two to the client or group as they work with the physical task of reaching, taking or letting go. Some examples of questions are:

What are you reaching towards? Now take something that you want from the centre of this group for yourself today. Now place something into the centre, something you can contribute to the group. What do you need to leave here today? How do you want to leave it? Are you throwing it? Shaking it off? Placing it down carefully for safe keeping?

Of course, this is not an exhaustive list of questions. The precise questions I ask will depend on my sense of what support the client or group needs in order to deepen their process. I may choose to ask no questions, or very few, if I feel that the task is to contain as much as possible rather than to gently begin the process of insight.

The process of taking, holding and letting go is one example of shaping or sculpting movement (see Chapter 2), whose purpose is adaptation to and influence on the environment. Shaping movements are thus intimately linked with issues of control and containment. The dance movement therapist can use creativity to enable clients to work with pertinent issues using shaping movements. Possible themes might include: swimming the rapids; moving through long grass; a tug of war; creating a sculpture of the perfect partner.

13 Shared Group Movement (circular formation)
One of the most commonly used techniques in group DMT is what is often referred to as shared group movement. Many of us will

know this as 'follow my leader'. The dance is usually performed in a circular formation because this structure both contains energy and reaffirms group identity. The following account illustrates the process:

> *I began a rhythmic movement for the group to follow. I invited each group member to do the movement in their own way, rather than to try to copy me exactly. I swayed from side to side, then introduced small arm movements. I looked around to check that everyone seemed to be interpreting the movement in their own way, without becoming lost or losing balance. Gradually, I made the movement bigger so that my arms took on a swing and my knees folded and unfolded to emphasise the rhythm in my whole body. Then after a while, I suggested that we pass the leadership around the circle, each group member taking a turn to lead the group unless they chose to pass the leadership straight on. I said that I would begin by passing to Stephen, who was on my left, and that we would continue on in that direction. I explained that, on taking the leadership, all that was required was to continue the movement that we had just been doing. If the leader wished to change the movement in any way, that was fine, but it wasn't necessary. No one had to 'think up' a movement. I hoped that in saying this I could avoid losing the flow within the circle and minimise stress. As each person took leadership, I gently encouraged them and reminded them of the task. When John took his turn, I reminded him by saying, 'Now we will do the movement John's way.' I also commented when it seemed that maybe John might be getting tired and might need to change the movement to accommodate this. I reflected what I saw, both verbally and non-verbally. I said that I noticed John was moving his hands as if he was passing something from one to the other. When Chris began to rub her hands rhythmically along her arms from top to bottom, one after the other, I wondered aloud whether she might be trying to get rid of something?*

For individual work, the process is similar to the example given above for group DMT. However, after I have led the movement for a while I generally follow the client, provided that the client is ready to lead me. If not, I continue to structure the movement but reflect on the client's unique interpretation of this.

14 Finding an Ending to the Improvisation

Some people find it difficult to allow a clear, organic ending to an improvisation. But when they do, it can give a sense of greater control and mastery over their emotions.

Brian tended to 'bury his head in the sand'. His philosophy on life was 'if I ignore it, it will go away'. It was only after a life crisis therefore that he was able to seek help. He found the expressive part of the movement embarassing. When he asked if he could sit down, I replied that of course he could, but could he find an ending to the movement first? He said that he wanted to let the cloth drop and sit down and forget about it. I remarked how this reminded me of his usual coping strategy, that was no longer working for him, and I suggested that maybe together we could find a way to end differently. He then noticed that he was feeling easier, having voiced his need to sit down and been heard. His movement took on a more organised, rhythmic quality. Eventually he gathered up his end of the cloth and handed it to me, marking a different kind of ending from the ones he had been used to in the past. He said he felt better after this and could see the point of what we were doing.

15 Choreography

Many dance movement therapists shy away from using choreographic structures or set steps in their work. However, I was inspired by an intensive four-day workshop I attended during the 1980s with Dr Marcia Leventhal in Leeds, England. She suggested that, following a long period of improvisation, we each construct a short movement motif that somehow crystallised our personal process. The work was further grounded through drawing an image, then discussing this in pairs with reference to our own movement. I found that this structure helped me to 'get a handle' on what I had been doing and to make sense of it in terms of my life and personal development. As a result, I often make use of my own version of this process with my clients.

I also use circle dances, both those choreographed from clients' own material and set circle dances. These can often be powerful markers of the ending of the session, containing feelings about endings and assisting in the transition. They thus serve a ritual function, rather like the rituals around birth, death, puberty and marriage that exist in our societies. They allow us to remain conscious while we process a transition, rather than to split off from the process or become overwhelmed by it. I would like to illustrate my use of circle dances through two short vignettes. The first illustrates the use of the group's own choreographed dance.

We stood in a circle, all women, all having suffered feelings of powerlessness. I suggested that we make a dance, by each contributing a movement that for us summed up an image of protection. One woman took a step backwards, placing her hands at the level of her hips, her palms facing backwards, fingers outstretched. She said she was protecting her children, so that they should not have to suffer as she had done. Another woman took up the stance of a warrior, arms braced before her face, ready either to deflect a blow or if necessary to attack. Her knees were bent, her stance wide to aid her stability. Each woman contributed her own unique movement, and the whole group echoed each movement in turn. At the end, we performed all of the movements together, finding easy transitions between them. Then I chose some music, a powerfully rhythmic piece based on Aboriginal American chants. As we continued to recycle the movements our dance took on a new energy. I asked the group what they wanted to call their dance and they chose the title 'Protection Warrior Dance'. After that, we often used the dance to mark either the beginning or end of a session, or when we felt in particular need of a reminder that we are both individually and collectively powerful as women.

My second case example shows the power of a set circle dance in marking a transition. This piece of work enabled one woman to metaphorically say goodbye to her dead baby.

Irene had lost a baby some years before, as a result of a rape. She decided it was time to say goodbye to the baby and asked for the group's help in this. We all brought something special to mark the occasion: a shawl, some flowers, medals of Our Lady from one woman with a Roman Catholic heritage. Irene held the doll that had become her dead baby, wrapped her in the shawl, and took her around the circle to each woman in turn. Some of the women took the baby, held her, cradled her in their arms. Others gently stroked her head,

saying a few words of blessing or prayer. All of us cried.
Then, Irene placed her baby on the cushion she had chosen,
surrounded by flowers and special things, and covered her up
for the last time. We all knew what we must now do. We had a
special circle dance that we always performed to mark the
end of each session. Now we danced the same dance to say
goodbye to Irene's baby.

Clinical Supervision

It is essential that dance movement therapists, like all other trained
therapists, receive clinical supervision for their work (Penfield,
1994). Models for this have often been adapted from the verbally
orientated therapies (described in, for example, Carroll, 1996). The
extent to which movement has been used has often been focused
on role play of the client (as described by Penfield, 1994) in order
to examine aspects of movement observation. However, more
recently some models have been proposed in which the creative
process is more central to supervision. Dance movement therapists
ask their clients to use movement to contact their unconscious.
Given that our responses to our clients encompass our somatic
(largely unconscious) countertransference it makes sense to move
in order to access, via the movement metaphor, what we unconsciously know about our clients and about our work. There are
usually archetypal themes governing this. I have found this 'movement supervision' approach to be a profound, quick and effective
way into the process. In the group supervision setting, I suggest
that group members give each other feedback, both as moving
witness and as stationary but aware witness, to deepen the individual therapist's perception of the process.

Penfield (1994) argues that the involvement of the therapist's
physical self in the interaction with the client means that countertransference can occur more immediately. She suggests that 'Protective structures must be developed to protect the emotional life
of therapists while releasing their kinesthetic skills to work for a
client' (1994: 4). She points out that since dance movement therapists often mirror the client's movement it is vital that they know
their own 'home base' to which they can return. Penfield also gives
some important advice concerning the role of supervisor, in that
the skills of the therapist are brought into play but within the
context of supporting the supervisee's professional growth and

focus on the client. I would argue that personal material is likely to come into this picture, as our reactions to our clients are not solely determined by their projections onto or into us. From time to time we have responses that have more to do with our own experience than that of the client. The role of supervision is, in part at least, to uncover these responses and make them conscious, so that we do not 'act out' on them but use them as a resource to deepen our understanding of the client. However, the supervisor must never lose sight of the client, nor of the therapist in the work context. Personal therapy (whose aim would be to aid the therapist as client) and clinical supervision (whose aim is to aid the therapist in assisting their client) should never be confused. Occasionally, it may be necessary for a clinical supervisor to recommend that the supervisee takes a particular issue to personal therapy when it is clear that further work needs to done within the goals of personal therapy.

Some dance movement therapists use other media in addition to movement during supervision. Penfield (1994) describes making use of drawing following a movement exploration, for example. Best (1999) describes a multi-modal approach to supervision influenced by systemic thinking. She argues that 'supervision for dance movement therapists, whatever the supporting psychotherapeutic theories, needs to take on board the personal creative "self" as being crucial to the professional "self"' (199: 17). She cites four core concepts in her supervision work:

1   Respect for difference.
2   Owning one's personal assumptions and prejudices.
3   Without a context there is no meaning
4   Mutual influence is inevitable within relationships.

Best argues that verbal supervision alone does not adequately address mutuality between dance movement therapist and client, and that movement should be located 'at the centre of the process' (1999: 19) in supervision.

Best discusses the phenomenon of reflection of the therapist's own physical or psychological issues within the therapy. She reveals that when she first noticed this in her own work she found it disconcerting, interpreting it as possibly a sign of incompetence. However, she offers an alternative view, that there are universal or collective themes into which both therapist and client enter. She suggests that one way to work with this phenomenon is for the therapist to maintain a reflexive stance. The supervisor helps the supervisee in this, in encouraging the exploration of alternative narratives about the client's life. Best shifts back and forth in supervision sessions between image and movement in order to aid this exploration. She warns supervisors that during role play supervisees will inevitably bring parts of themselves into the action, and that this must be recognised to avoid false interpretations about the client's experience. Nevertheless, Best maintains a firm belief in the power of improvised movement as a source of wisdom both within the DMT session and in supervision. She reminds us that 'the "dance" between client and therapist, and between the movements, images and metaphors, "speaks" in a way which can not always be reached through cognitive, analytic means' (1999: 25). Best therefore proposes four 'core ideas' in relation to the supervision of arts therapists (1999: 25):

1 Paying attention to the creative imagery of the therapist.
2 The value of sensory wisdom and bodily knowledge.
3 The central place of improvisation within the therapeutic relationship (and presumably therefore in supervision).
4 The importance of dancing between body experience, image and word as ways of creating new narratives and new ways of being in the world.

My own approach has been developed through a long collaboration with my colleague Susan Boon Scarth. Susan has written about our approach elsewhere (Scarth, 1995). We tend to start supervision sessions with some brief dialogue to set the scene, but without creating an agenda. We then warm up our bodies and move into improvisation. This improvisatory state demands at once both an allowing of the impulse to move without attempting to become analytical and the maintenance of an observer stance. The reason that I try to avoid becoming too analytical at this stage is that I feel it would close down my inquiry too soon. I allow my body to speak in metaphor, the wisdom it needs to impart to me. I move with an openness to my own imagery, but with the express intention of shedding light on my work as a dance movement therapist. When I feel that my movement has in essence come close to completing its dance (movement being the building blocks, the dance being the gestalt), then I will often consciously work towards finding a movement motif, a short phrase that in essence sums up my dance. As described above, I learned to do this in my work with Dr Leventhal. Best (1999) refers to a similar practice. It is often at this stage, though sometimes not until later when I sit on a chair or cushion to discuss my movement, that the metaphorical signifi-cance of my movement and its link with my work becomes apparent. I think that this transition from movement to stillness and an upright position is important, as it engages left brain (rational/linguistic) activity and forms a link between this and the right brain (intuitive, creative/affective) activity used during dance improvisation.

Despite the fact that Susan Scarth and I did not collectively discuss our approach with Penelope Best, it is surprisingly similar to hers, although our images have largely been expressed through movement and words and have not included drawing. This has not been a conscious omission, as personally I have often used draw-ings as a way of dialoguing with my imagery, developing my movement information and vice versa. I have also used drawings with some of my other supervisees.

Some time after I began working with Susan Scarth, I had some experience of a multi-arts group supervision approach used by Paul Wilkins (1995). His approach derives from his training as a person-centred psychodramatist and incorporates some techniques from art therapy. The strength of psychodrama as a supervisory tool lies in part in its active use of the group context. Supervision in groups becomes less of a time-sharing exercise and more of a collaborative approach in which the group is an important resource for the supervisee. The structures inherent in psycho-drama allow not only for a deeper understanding of both client and therapist but also can be used to practice new ways of being with the client. Some of the suggestions for these experiments can come from the 'audience'. Wilkins' description of psychodrama in this setting emphasises its role in problem solving, especially when the supervisee is feeling 'stuck'. He also points to the usefulness of the approach in addressing 'unfinished business' after a client has ended work with the therapist. As with the approaches to DMT supervision used by myself and Susan Scarth, and by Penelope Best described above, the creative process is exploited to its fullest in allowing the natural wisdom (right brain and left brain) of the therapist and supervisor/group to emerge.

Movement Profiles in the Early Phase of DMT

I have recently carried out a small investigation with respect to one DMT group that I facilitated in a community mental health setting.

There were three participants in the group, one of whom joined half way through. The group was time limited, for six months, and aimed at addressing pre-discharge issues, including attachment and loss. Although designed to be a mixed group, the membership was in fact all women. The single gender inevitably influenced the issues addressed in therapy. All of the women were suffering from mental health symptoms associated with childhood trauma. Most of the sessions were videotaped, with the women's consent. After the group had ended, I chose sections of the tapes that would enable me to investigate the women's movement profiles. For the two women who had been present throughout, I chose tapes that were at the beginning, middle and end. For the third woman I chose tapes for her own beginning (the middle of the group) and the end. Each section of tape chosen was one minute long. I coded the tapes so that I could not immediately identify them, and delivered instructions to myself for viewing them, which were also issued to a second rater (her data are not available at the time of writing). She would be viewing the tapes without knowing which section related to what stage in the therapy. In the event, when I got around to viewing them (10 months after the end of the group) I had also forgotten what stages they referred to until I looked at my observations with reference to my coding sheet for the tapes.

This was by no means a flawless scientific study. I used a very small sample and was myself both therapist, selector and coder of tapes, and also observer. Nevertheless what I observed was interesting. It remains for my findings to be confirmed by an outside observer. In the description that follows, I shall refer to the women as Anne, Brenda and Carol. Carol is the one who joined half-way through, knowing neither of the other women beforehand. Anne and Brenda had previous experience together of being in a DMT group with me, and Carol had been in individual DMT with me.

At the start of the group, despite both of the women having been in group DMT with me before, I noticed that Anne used a lot of sustainment in her actions, along with strong Weight and both Direct and Flexible use of Space (North, 1972). This seemed to add up to considered action. Her movement phrases were rhythmic, starting off with Strong, Direct and Sudden and moving into Light, Flexible and Sustained. This latter (an indulgence in Time, Space and Weight) can be seen as the recovery action for the first (fighting Time, Space and Weight). Her eye contact was at times fleeting, at other times flexible. I noticed the use of what Kestenberg (Kestenberg and Sossin, 1979) terms 'inner genital libidinal rhythms', like slowly undulating ocean waves. My sense of her was that she was dipping her toes in the water, then indulging in the joy of it.

With Brenda, on the other hand, there was no hesitancy at all in taking something in and being nourished by it. She made a lot of gathering movements towards her body and displayed a strong, controlled mastery of the environment in her use of sculpting movements, often on the 'table plane' (using Space in a horizontal area around the waist) associated with relating. There was occasional use of Shape Flow, which is developmentally a much earlier movement associated with the infant's total dependency. The rhythm of these movements was also oral libidinal (Kestenberg and Sossin, 1979), associated with early stages of development. There was very little decision in her mastery, as indicated by the absence of the Time Effort. Again, this could be considered to be consistent with early stages of development. It seemed that she was trying to get, through the group, the kind of love and care that she had not received when very young.

Carol showed a clear split between the upper and lower portions of her body, the lower being far more strongly held than the upper, in her first session. She unsurprisingly used a lot of Bound Flow and Sustainment, which are consistent with a careful, considered attitude that I guess most of us would have when entering a group that is already established. She was hesitant about making eye contact, and her movements were all initiated by the centre of her body with little peripheral involvement. There was a twisting, wringing quality to the movement ('anal libidinal', Kestenberg and Sossin, 1979) that is associated with the stage of development to do with becoming a separate person and asserting oneself. My sense of her was of someone not yet putting herself out there. She was working for herself, keeping it all in and not letting go.

Summary

In this chapter I have described the beginning phase of dance movement therapy. We have spent some time looking at how I conduct formal assessments, considered issues of personal safety, discussed the importance of the therapeutic relationship and proceeded to clinical applications in this phase. I have emphasised the containing functions of DMT which are particularly relevant to this phase of the therapy. However, these are by no means exclusive to the early part of DMT, and may in some cases provide the sole focus for therapy. Containment is certainly revisited at other times during the therapy, as and when it is needed. One such occasion is towards the end of therapy, as Chapter 5 will illustrate. But for now, we will proceed to the middle phase of therapy.

Notes

1 The warm-up is described later in this chapter.
2 The creative/symbolic part of the DMT session is described in detail in Chapter 4.

4

INCUBATION AND ILLUMINATION: LETTING GO INTO THE DARKNESS AND SEEING A LIGHT

I was giving movement supervision to a group of practitioners, when I was struck by two images that emerged in the group movement process. One image was of the whole group sitting, appearing to hold something very large in their arms, the lower half of their bodies apparently sliding away, as if disconnected from the experience of the upper body. The other image was of half the group rolling on the floor like babies of a few months old, whilst the other half stood upright, reaching upwards with their arms.

A discussion ensued. Some of the supervisees shared difficulties with transitions, tending to see their experience in all-or-nothing terms rather than the shades in between. Others spoke of their tendency to merge with other human beings. Some spoke of recent motherhood and of the need both to spend time with their offspring and to be their own person. Several, reflecting on their clients' experience of DMT, spoke of the fear of fragmentation and invasion, particularly in the potentially exposing experience of moving in the space, where one's true feelings and cognitions may be revealed. This seemed at odds with the need to be witnessed, held, contained, embodied. In the embodied self, it seemed, the disparate parts of the psyche could be synthesised and made whole. One woman was aware of her wish to be 'all grown up' and stand on her own two feet, but at odds with this was her desire and need to reconnect with the past, and her need to merge. She eventually gave into this impulse, rolled on the floor, and found a comfortable way to get up that did not jar with her own needs.

Prior to this movement experience, the group members had been reflecting on their geographical distance from each other, their need to be accepted in the face of diversity, and their wish to make meaningful connections with each other. It occurred to me that the two images that had struck me had summed up their process. In the first image, the group struggled with the seemingly opposite needs for, on the one hand, being held and accepted, integrated into some kind of whole and on the other, being oneself, sliding away from being contained. The second image showed clearly the developmental dilemma; in order to be grown up and separate we must first of all merge, bond, be small. Otherwise we risk becoming falsely self-reliant. The development of the individual is from dependence towards *inter*dependence, rather than independence (Winnicott, 1963).

Letting Go into the Darkness

In the DMT process, clients similarly often go through a merging with the therapist in this middle phase of the therapy before developing in the way they need to and moving away. There is a quality of 'letting go' of controls in this phase, characterised by more risk taking on the part of the client. Secrets may emerge, including events that the client finds deeply embarrassing or painful.

The handling of this process requires great skill on the part of the therapist. Clinical supervision is of course essential. The therapist may experience feelings that somehow reflect or empathise with the client's experience. For example, in an in-patient group I ran recently the emerging theme was one of loss or fear of loss, and the need to be with loved ones. More than one person in the group began wailing. I was instantly reminded of my own experiences of loss, and the recent near loss of a loved one. My guts yearned along with them. At times like this, the therapist needs to be able to recognise and then set aside personal material, whilst also keeping it available as a resource if needed in the service of the therapy.

During this phase of the work, the client will seem to dip in and out of active work. It is not possible to keep up the intensity brought by this deep descent into the unconscious. Hence the client not only dances towards and away from the therapist, but towards and away from the Self.

This phase of the group process is also one in which the group tends to gel to greater or lesser degrees. Sometimes this can be seen in unconscious mirroring. One way to deepen the strength of the group is to suggest that they all sense together the time to stop or start a movement, for example walking across a diagonal together in the studio. Endings of group sessions take on a new feel. They may involve hand holding, humming, stillness, rocking or singing, or any combination of these.

Dance Movement Therapist as Active Agent

Since the contents of the unconscious are rich in symbols, this phase of the work also contains a wealth of spontaneous movement metaphors. The role of the therapist is in many ways less active than in the early phase of therapy, providing more open-ended structures in which the client can explore personally meaningful metaphors. However, this does not mean that the therapist becomes passive. The process demands a vigilant awareness and a readiness to provide safety, containment and structure whenever needed. But above all, the therapist needs to be fully present, as empathic witness to the client's dance. It is then for the client to discover the meaning behind the symbolism contained within the dance. The therapist's task is to ask open-ended questions, provide a theme for dance improvisation (emerging from the ongoing process) and reflect from the perspective of witness. Some of the themes for dance movement improvisation I have used in this stage of therapy are: choice; being seen; giving voice; meeting and parting; opening and closing; going at your own pace; descending into the darkness; dungeons and dragons; finding your own way; grasping the nettle;[1] letting go; sharing space; power and strength; mirroring; senses; body parts; wanting elbow room; waking up; handling it; keeping yourself together.

Dance Movement Therapist as Co-creator

Props provide one way of allowing insight to remain at the level of the metaphor, and thus protecting the individual from the impact of full conscious awareness. The therapist's ability to work with this metaphoric material is an important skill.

Jennifer chose to work with a large balloon. As she handled it, she observed that it did not have as much air in it as when it was first blown up. Yet, when she said this, it sounded to me as if she would say 'when it was first born'.

I internally questioned my 'hunch'. I wondered if it might be that this was due to my (rudimentary) knowledge about her past. Was I projecting something onto her? I knew she was a survivor of childhood abuse, and that maybe the air symbolised her spirit. Maybe she felt that some of her spirit had been lost by the events since her birth. Was I in fact finely tuned into her symbolism? She did seem to hesitate around the word 'blown', pronouncing the 'b' and then waiting to form the rest of the word.

I am intrigued by the role of the therapist. Are we co-creators or mirrors? How much of ourselves do we bring to the encounter? Should we be pure vessels, waiting to be filled by the client's mysteries, or is the personhood that we bring to the encounter an important part of the process? Is there a larger plan into which we both fit? I do not have answers to these questions, though I feel the questions themselves to be important. I do feel it is possible that my client and I belong to a larger sphere of existence than that of our conscious and individual minds. I also know that I must constantly check through reflexive practice and clinical supervision whether my own personal material is getting in the way of the client's growth. I must not allow any beliefs I have about my perceptions in relation to a wider collective consciousness to become an excuse for grandiosity. The client's own perception is the important one. I do not in fact know what is going to emerge during this phase of therapy. It is exciting and scary for me. I 'fly by the seat of my pants', and remind myself of the power of this work (not of myself!) in order to remain open and available to the client's process as it unfolds.

When facilitating groups with people in acute ward-based settings, I have been struck by the fact that my co-worker and I have in some way 'held' the notion of the group (Sandel and Johnson, 1983), when the group itself did not exist as any ongoing entity within the minds of group members. Each group member may only attend once or twice. At the end of a twelve week period in such a group it is likely that no-one in the group will have been present at the beginning. Yet my co-worker and I have the sense of some kind of thread. The themes seem to link from week to week, so that not every session is a new beginning. Is this my and my co-worker's need to make sense of what we are doing, to make it meaningful beyond the immediate encounter? Or is something else at work here? Do we in fact, as co-creators of this group, hold that entity in our psyches so that new members can merge with it? Is it similar to the role of the mother who, knowing her infant to be a separate human being from herself even though the infant does not yet have a concept of self and other, calls the infant by name and holds the body parts in one whole, responding to every sign of distress or pleasure?

Methods of Working

A DMT session that includes some symbolic work can take one of several formats. Levy (1992) describes the different approaches of the major American pioneers. One approach, loosely based on the work of Marian Chace (one of the American pioneers), will begin with a physical warm-up, like that described in Chapter 3. From the warm-up, the group may move into what is often termed 'shared leadership'. This may focus on a prop shared by the whole group, for example, or movement could take the form of 'follow my leader'. The group maintains the containing structure of the circle, whilst allowing for individual and group imagery to emerge.

It is the middle section of both the session and of the therapy as a whole, in which the process deepens, that concerns us in this chapter. In general, this work more overtly makes use of the client's own metaphors than in the preparation/warm-up phase described in the previous chapter.

My own approach to working with clients is flexible, depending on the needs of the group. I sometimes use a quasi-Chacian approach and at other times I set up exploratory exercises planned in response to group process.

This may take one of several forms. For example:

1 An individual client might take the lead in a continuation of the warm-up, either with the same music or with a different piece of music (this can be chosen by the client). My role here would be to follow the movement and reflect it non-verbally, as a way of showing that I am 'with' the client. I might also respond by reflecting some quality in the movement, rather than precisely copying, as a way of drawing the client's attention to this quality. Or I might augment or diminish the movement in some way, for example by taking up more or less space, often working with qualitative polarities like big/little, fast/slow within the movement, again as a way of drawing attention to a continuum of possibilities.

2 The client or group may want to work with one of the props that I keep in the studio.

3 We may work together on a symbolic aspect of verbal check-in or of the warm-up, or an emerging theme from the previous session. For example, I may suggest reaching for something that is just beyond the client's preferred sphere of action.

4 I may sit outside of the movement area, on a chair, and give an individual client the opportunity to move without either interruptions or the need to relate to me. The option is given of moving with eyes open or shut. My role here is to witness the client's movement and to maintain the boundaries of safety and timing. My approach is adapted from my training in 'release work' (Fulkerson, 1982) but has some elements in common with Authentic Movement™. The following case example illustrates this more open-ended, improvisatory structure.

Ruth took up a position near the window, and shut her eyes. I remained seated, to give her the space, and adopted a quiet, respectful, waiting attitude.[2] Slowly, she began to rock from side to side, hiding her hands behind her back. I could just see her hands. Their rhythm was entirely different from her whole body action. They showed me her 'shadow movement' (North, 1972) of wringing and twisting. She began to cry. Afterwards, when I asked her about this movement she said that when talking to her parents she had always hidden her hands behind her back and wrung them, to avoid showing her feelings.

A *Safety Line*

Facing the really scary bits can be made possible by reaffirming sources of support and safety. Props can help to make the process safer because they enable the individual and group to project feelings, memories and associations onto something external. Sometimes this can work in surprising and playful ways.

Carole found that working with a brightly coloured parachute enabled her to play a game of hiding. This led to her remembering that her father allowed her to be herself, whereas her son does not. The struggle to realise that she is loveable continued right up to the end of the group for Carole. It was knowing that the other women wanted to continue meeting with her, and their weekly witnessing of her movement, that enabled Carole finally to see that she was indeed loveable.

Sometimes, working on aggression can be easier for the group than working on bonding. This is especially true when one considers that many of the clients of child and adolescent mental health services have suffered childhood abuse.

I had been working with a group of adolescents for about ten sessions. I noticed that structures that involved touch between participants were problematic. Some of the group members would sit out. Some would say they did not like touching, but then hang around as if hoping to be touched. Others would talk openly about having been beaten or about fears of loss of loved ones. One week, I decided to work with shadow fighting in pairs. The rule was very clear: one makes a move, then the other, and so on. And no contact. Afterwards, several of the young people said that it had been much easier this week, because the fighting had clear limits, whereas affection does not. The following week, we worked on mirroring each other's movements in pairs (the limit of no touch being very clear). One of the young men, partnering a female worker, led the movement in such a way that it was obvious he was trying to get her to touch herself in private parts of her body. She of course refused to do so, explaining that these parts of her body were private and not to be touched in the group by anybody. Another young man had a positive experience. Partnering a male member of staff for the duet, he said afterwards that it was like having a really good friend.

The Movement Metaphor and Ongoing Assessment

I was working with a group of adolescents, and made it clear that I kept notes on each session. I told the group that if anyone wanted me to read out what I had written about them I would do so, though I would not read what I had written about anyone else in the group to that individual. I had noted on one occasion that when we were passing a movement around the circle, Charlene was offered some food in a mime by the person next to her. She instantly changed it to something else, without responding to it as if it were food. Some weeks later, she came up to me and asked to hear what I had written so far about her. When I came to the section about the food mime, she told me that she avoids food.

The above example illustrates the role of the movement metaphor in ongoing assessment. Assessment does not stop as therapy starts, though it particularly features before or at the beginning of therapy. This initial assessment can play an important part in establishing a therapeutic relationship. A further example of how movement metaphors can give ongoing information to both therapist and client is provided from the following work with a mother and her small child:

The group decided to build an environment, using cloth and chairs and whatever was lying around. The environment had many obstacles and scary places. The task was to journey through this terrain and arrive at a place of safety. Most of the mothers were more or less protective of their young children as they journeyed together. However, when Sarah arrived with her little girl Stephanie at the place where the snakes dwelled, she stood by and watched as her little girl entered.

I have witnessed several further examples of the richness of movement metaphor in ongoing assessment of family systems.

Perhaps it is because children instinctively understand the language of metaphor through play. Or maybe I have learned to tune in to that material. The following example links the movement metaphor to family movement observation systems developed through systematic research (Dulicai, 1977; Meekums, 1990, 1991, 1992).

Sharon talked a lot about not being able to breathe. In one session, the children began using large bean bags to cover people and be covered. I encouraged the mothers to 'find' their hidden children. Several of the women were slow to respond to this suggestion, but Sharon pulled her daughter Charlene out quickly. I wondered privately whether this had anything to do with her own difficulties with breathing rather than her fears for her child's safety. As she pulled Charlene out, I realised that she had her daughter by one wrist only. She tried to catch her little one in both arms, but missed and dropped her.

Staying at the Level of Metaphor

It is not always necessary to intellectually process the metaphoric language inherent in the DMT process. The following case example illustrates work with someone who has bipolar disorder (manic depression). Bipolar disorder is characterised by extremes of mood. Typically, the person will at times be depressed, and at other times be 'high'. These high phases may result in disinhibited behaviour, including unnecessary and expensive purchases or aggressive outbursts.

I had been working for a few months with Hilda. She chose a sari cloth to move with. As we moved together, Hilda remarked that at times it was like being up in the clouds, and then under a cloud. I was struck by the metaphoric link between these expressions and first elation then depression. However, I did not bring this to Hilda's attention, choosing instead to show her that I had heard and understood by reflecting her words back to her and allowing her to direct the process.

Sometimes even the therapist does not consciously spot the symbolism, yet still responds to it.

I was working with a group of mothers and young children. Shaheen and her two-year-old son Jamil were moving together, he lying on her back while she crawled around the floor. They looked very comfortable together. Then, Shaheen started to move as if she wished to get up. I noticed this, and swiftly went over to show her how to get the child off her back without hurting him, reaching round to hold him in place and then allowing him to slide to his feet on the floor. I happened to have Sherry Goodill, ADTR in the group that day, giving me live supervision. After the session, she told me that she was intrigued by how I had worked with the metaphor of 'getting the child off your back'. I had not previously seen the significance of this.

In acute ward-based settings, clients may only attend once or twice before discharge. Such very brief interventions are not conducive to insight-orientated therapies. It would be irresponsible of any therapist to make conscious the client's symbolism and then leave the person struggling with this insight, with nowhere to process it. Working with people who have psychosis, the metaphors can at times flow thick and fast. It is as if the individual is connected to a very rich, archetypal and magical world, in which to name the symbolism would be to destroy its power. Sometimes I do not feel that I fully understand the metaphor, but at the same time I do not need to consciously understand, since the client has not made the metaphor conscious. What is important is that I enter into the world of symbolism with the client. The following example may in fact be an indicator of the wish to be contained inside the therapist's psyche, as in the phenomenon referred to as 'transference'. It also shows a shift from delusional fantasy to metaphor. However, whilst the shift in delusional belief appears dramatic, it is not known whether this persisted. Delusional beliefs are tenacious, and it is important for therapists to avoid messianic interpretations of their own work (Sandel, 1980).

Richard held a hollow instrument in his hands, upside down. He gave it a sharp thump, and then looked at me and said: 'That's you, I'm inside your head'. After the session was over he remarked that he had said similar things for the past five years, but that today in the group he had realised that he could not get inside my head. He concluded that his beliefs were due to a mental illness, rather than being based in 'reality'.

Dance Movement Therapy and Role

Dance as an art form encompasses many aspects of theatre, including role and the use of props. Dance movement therapy sometimes allows participants to enact roles, rather as in drama-therapy. This provides some concealment for the client and allows for experimentation with new ways of being.

Derek's demeanour could be characterised as passive aggression. He would speak very quietly, hardly ever making eye contact, and wait for props to be passed to him rather than reaching out. My own countertransference was of irritation with him. I knew that this signalled the possibility that he might in fact be angry, though I had no idea what about. He seemed disempowered. On one occasion, my co-worker suggested that the group members might choose a prop from a number of pieces of cloth. He chose a red cloth, and this time he reached out and took it himself from the pile of cloths in the centre of the room. Still sitting, he positioned the cloth beside him and declared that he was a toreodor! The phrase 'red rag to a bull' came into my mind, and I realised why I had felt irritated by him. I did not need to understand the origin of his anger, but in that instant I was able to support its expression within the container of his chosen role.

The Body Doesn't Lie

The body can contain information about important object relationships (relationships with significant others in childhood) in the way that physical symptoms develop. The following case example demonstrates this.

Joe was a counsellor who had helped some of the families of victims following a national disaster that involved people being crushed as they tried to escape. His presenting problem was that his energy would tend to drain on Saturdays and he did not know why. We agreed to work together for five sessions. Joe was more than happy to accept that such a short-term contract would mean he must work on issues between sessions.

Joe had himself had the experience of nearly being crushed some time before the incident, and he also had asthma. He was surprised to find that we were meeting in an attic, having expected it to be a basement.

As we worked together, I noticed that Joe had a coughing fit whenever things seemed to shift on an emotional level. As he coughed, he would cross one forearm across his stomach and bring the other hand up to his mouth. The whole effect was a kind of narrowing or constriction in the body. I also learned that he tended to eat to push down emotions as they surfaced.

The other thing I noticed about Joe was his tendency to push himself to face fear and to achieve goals. As we worked together, it emerged that asthma attacks were one of Joe's few sources of parental attention as a child. He remembered also having tantrums when out shopping with his mother on Saturdays (the day of the week on which the disaster had occurred and on which his energy would now drain).

The following example illustrates how the issues that the client brings can be powerfully played out in the therapeutic movement relationship.

Shelley told me that she had fears of being hurt and of hurting others. As she improvised, I mirrored her movements. Her arms were crossed. She reflected that my mirrored stance looked as if she had chopped off both of my arms.

Unfinished Business

Occasionally, a dance improvisation may be used by a client for the purpose of resolving some 'unfinished business'.

Gail was moving to some music chosen by the group. I could see her hugging herself and rocking. Then, it was as if something slipped out of her arms. I became aware of a feeling of sadness. Afterwards, during the verbal processing,

Gail told us that she had been in the waves and had let go of a (dead) loved one, watching him float away on the water. She felt calm, and knew she must let go, both of him and of her long held-in tears.

There are several things about this that I find interesting. First, I had no idea what Ruth was imagining while dancing, although I could tell that she was deeply engrossed in some internal imagery. Secondly, the rhythm of waves lapping is what Judith Kestenberg (Kestenberg and Sossin, 1979), a child psychiatrist, calls the 'oral rhythm', associated with mother–child bonding, and often used at times when we need comfort (as in rocking). Thirdly, the image of the sea is a very powerful one, it being a container of unseen depths and often associated linguistically with the concept of 'mother' as in the French *la mère* (the mother) and *la mer* (the sea).

The following case example also links to loss issues. It addresses the importance of acknowledging coping strategies that may have a degree of usefulness, whilst not fully meeting the needs of the individual in the present.

Freda tended to push herself. She moved harder and faster than the other women in the group. It was important to her to keep fit, to stay ahead, so that no one could catch and harm her. The problem was that no matter how hard she pushed herself, she could not escape the ghosts of her past.

One of the ways Freda would push herself was to give to others, but to avoid receiving. The gifts she gave were plants, lovingly tended from cuttings; they seemed to be metaphors for her own need to be nurtured. She found it hurtful when the people she gave these plants to failed to look after them properly. Nevertheless, she received enough thanks to rein-force her giving and to contribute positively to her self-esteem and her sense of herself as strong.

Physically, Freda's body seemed to be 'split', with her upper and lower torso working against each other. She had not learned to soften in the knees or to use the floor as a friend. She seemed to be fighting her one source of sure support. Reaching down and giving in to gravity seemed to be associated with the dark past, and with defeat.

Eventually, Freda admitted to the group that she felt lost. She blamed herself for 'getting it wrong' and began kicking out, blindly attacking the spectre of men who had hurt her. She was unable cognitively to separate these attackers from men as a whole. As Freda began to trust the other women in the group, she slowly accepted that the only way to move forward was to stop fighting her feelings. This meant accepting her (albeit irrational) anger with her own mother for dying when she was a little girl and leaving her vulnerable, as well as her anger with the man who had abused her.

Risking Change

DMT can be used to explore issues linked to behavioural, cognitive and affective change. The richness of metaphor allows for scenarios to be explored before risking any change in the 'real' world.

Sarah had a brother, who was misusing alcohol. Every time he ran out of money, he would come to Sarah and ask for more. She was not wealthy, although she worked hard and felt responsible for him, the little brother. She had always played a protective role in his life, since their own mother was often unavailable to them when they were younger. Every time Sarah's brother asked for money, he had a plausible excuse, and so Sarah generally gave in. But he kept on drinking.

I suggested Sarah might like to choose an object in the room to represent her brother. She chose a South American rain stick that was leaning against a wall, and instantly recognised this as like her brother, who was slightly built while she was somewhat overweight. I suggested we move over to the centre of the space, and I brought the rain stick to her there. We together observed that the stick could not stand up on its own and needed to be supported. It was not possible for Sarah to lean on the stick to any great degree, without both the stick and her losing their balance. Then I noticed that if she continually held the stick it was never going to get the experience of finding its own balance. I wondered what would happen if she carefully balanced the stick and then stood back a little, without going away completely. She tried this, and the stick balanced for a short while. It toppled shortly, and Sarah was again able to balance the stick and retreat. This happened several times.

We discussed what all of this meant for Sarah. She herself concluded that if she kept on holding up her brother he was never going to find his own balance. She knew that she now had to frustrate his desire for her to rescue him, because this was not in fact helpful for him in the long run. She resolved that whenever he asked for money in the future she would help him to see how he could solve his problem, but she would not solve it for him. From that day forward, she changed her behaviour towards her brother and as a result her own mental health improved. I did not hear how her brother was getting on.

Behavioural change may be more closely linked to feelings about oneself than relationships.

Avril hated her body. She had had breast reduction surgery, but was still dissatisfied with herself. She had received little love from either of her parents, and had passed on her mother's ambivalence about motherhood in her relationship with her own child. She spent a lot of her life doing battle with all and sundry. Avril chose a large physiotherapy ball to work with, that reminded her of a huge breast. After a while, she lay on top of the ball and became much more relaxed than I had previously seen her. It seemed to me that she was at last able to take something positive from the breast. Towards the end of her therapy, Avril told me that the experience had been a turning point. She was no longer so angry, and was able to recall the physical image and feelings of peace associated with lying on top of the ball. In moments of agitation, she would recall this moment and thereby calm herself.

Sometimes, the metaphoric nature of DMT can be used to explore issues using small movements whilst seated, as the following example illustrates.

Samantha had been sexually abused as a child. When she was telling me something particularly painful, she would hold onto a small rubber ball that lay around the studio. I noticed the ball was becoming dirty. One week I also had to hand a clean, bright, new version of the same prop. Samantha refused at first to hold the new ball, for fear of contaminating it. She said she could hold the dirty ball because it was like her. Gradually, we worked with holding both balls and then accepting the new ball. Eventually, she was able to accept the possibility that she herself was not soiled and would not contaminate whatever she came into contact with.

Embodying Relationships

I have previously described (Meekums, 1988) some family and marital work with Mr and Mrs W. The following is a précis of this work.

Mr W had been a heavy drinker, but was now teetotal. When he stopped drinking, his wife came to rely on him to control the children and perform various tasks around the home. In their first marital session, Mr and Mrs W were discussing their lack of mutual support, and so I set up some leaning activities. They managed to lean into each other when standing, but counterbalancing each other's weight when leaning outwards was more difficult. Mr W seemed hesitant, a fact that did not escape his wife's attention. She observed that he was scared she would fall. When they sat and moved together back to back, Mr W observed that they were unable to co-ordinate their movements. Mrs W leaned quite easily on him, but his own movements were hesitant and jerky. This dynamic was explored with the couple, who developed new ways of being with each other in movement. This change was then visible in DMT sessions with the whole family. The couple observed in their review interview that marital DMT had enabled them to co-ordinate their efforts with the children.

A Changing Sense of Self

Some clients have anxieties about their own power and sense that they might contact this during DMT sessions. However, a movement process that enables the client to contact personal power can facilitate the shift from victim to victor.

Jenny had been sexually abused in childhood, by a family member. She had a bodily sensation that recurred during moments of anxiety, that she described as a 'whoosh'. I asked her if she could go with this sensation in movement, and she

*told me she was afraid that she would lose control if she did
so. I suggested that we both hold onto a stretch cloth. Initially,
she responded with passive Weight, that is she had a defeated
feel to her energy, like someone slumped in a chair or
walking with exhaustion. I encouraged her to pull at the
cloth, against me. She did so, but held her breath, so I
encouraged her to breathe and move at the same time. She
began to introduce movements of wringing the cloth, then
flapping it up and down, and wrapping it over to one side
and then the other. She began to growl, initially strangling
the sound in her throat and then eventually with my encouragement letting the sound come from her belly. She laughed a
lot at this point, too. She began to tug more at the cloth, to
which I responded by verbalising what I felt she was saying
with her movement: 'Give it to me!' My hunch was confirmed
by her enthusiastically joining in with this verbalisation.
She carried on moving energetically, until she became tired
and decided to rest. She realised that she had not lost control,
but rather had both expressed and contained her feelings at
the same time. She told me that when she was letting the cloth
rise and fall she had imagined letting the cloth fall on the
abuser and pressing it down on him.*

Reconnecting with Play

For some people, DMT helps them not only to face difficult and
painful emotions but also to rediscover their playful selves, to
reconnect with that part of the developing individual that is healthy
and creative. Because so much of our play as children involves
sensori-motor activity, movement provides a useful bridge to the
essence of our cultural life. Often, images of childhood play will
emerge quite spontaneously. One way to access this is by working
on different levels (high, middle and low), which might bring
memories of running races, rolling down grassy banks or climbing
trees. Another way is to work with different environments. I often
use both large and small objects in my work and suggest that the
individual or group prepares, then moves through an environment
of their choosing. Pieces of blue cloth become lagoons, green
cushions become grass, a stage becomes a tree to climb, a piece of
cloth draped over two chairs becomes a cave in which the client
can hide or may confront dragons and demons. It is important to

support this process by asking appropriate questions when necessary, for example 'what could this piece of cloth be used for/what does it remind you of?' It is also important not to influence too much, only intervening if necessary to assist in a task required by the client.

Movement Profiles in the Middle Phase of DMT

In the previous chapter, I introduced some movement observation I have performed from videotaped sessions of one particular group. Details of the methodology are in Chapter 3. I would like to continue here by describing what I observed from videotapes of Anne and Brenda approximately half way through the group.

Anne was by now using high, medium and low levels in space. My sense was of her taking in nurturance with strength, care (Bound Flow) and thoroughness (an all-round attention in her use of Space). She would do this with a reaching out and gathering action on the 'table plane' (horizontally in relation to the torso), denoting relationship. She seemed firmly centred in her self. Once having gathered, she would hold with a kind of careful moulding, three-dimensionality, indulging in the moment and rocking almost as in a memory of something long past.

Brenda seemed to be displaying a split between her upper and lower body, in that they were not moving in harmony with each other. The lower half of her body was quite held, and she used predominantly gestural movements, that is ones that had no connection to the centre of her body. This alternated with whole-body, postural movements but posture and gesture were not merged. We would normally see posture–gesture merging (Lamb, 1965; Lamb and Watson, 1979) as 'ripple effects'. For example, if I begin to smile (a facial gesture), and then laugh (still a gesture, though beginning to involve other parts of my body including my breathing apparatus), I might also cross my arms and sink back into my chair, as if amused by some thought or by what I have seen. The sinking back into my chair is a posture, and the flow between all of these actions is posture–gesture merging. Lamb suggests that this phenomenon denotes a commitment to the action, and so we might conclude that Brenda was less committed to her actions within the group on this particular day. The phrasing of her movements was impulsive, in that it had Strength and Directness and Suddenness at the beginning of the phrase, followed by the recovery offered by Sustainment and Flexible use of Space. This was seen in her use of a stretch cloth, which she tossed in the air and then allowed to float down. Given the impulsivity in her actions, it is perhaps just as well that this did not have full postural back-up. However, the upward action mitigates to some extent against the Strength with which she tossed the cloth in the air, since Strength has an affinity with downward action. My sense of Brenda was thus of someone withholding her anger, perhaps with some justification. The rhythm of her action was what Kestenberg (Kestenberg and Sossin, 1979) calls 'phallic aggressive', associated with the action of leaping and with pubescence.

Summary

In this chapter, we have examined the middle phase in the DMT process. This has included the metaphor of a descent into a dark place and the emergence into the light. We have looked at the role of the therapist as active agent and co-creator. Methods of working have broadly encompassed several forms including a quasi-Chacian approach (shared movement), structured improvisations and free improvisations. We have also examined the ongoing need for safety and the role of metaphor, both in ongoing assessment and in DMT process. A brief consideration was given to the use of role in DMT. We then went on to look at the potential for DMT in working with unfinished business, psychological change, relationships, a changing sense of self, and reconnecting to playfulness. Finally, we looked at some movement profiles from this stage in therapy. In the next chapter, we will move on to endings.

Notes

1 With thanks to Dr Jaya Gowrisunkur, consultant psychotherapist, for this metaphor.
2 Mary Fulkerson, who taught me release work, used to call this 'waiting without expectation'.

5

EVALUATION: THE FINAL CAMPFIRE

When I suggested to my women's DMT group that we might look towards an ending, it brought some very strong reactions. All of the women had faced precipitous endings in their lives, endings over which they had no control. I was determined that this group would both give them an opportunity to face their feelings about that and give them a different experience. They reacted by not turning up to the next session!

However, when they did return, Jyoti was able to say how difficult it was for her to express any anger, because her experience had been that people get hurt and even die when she expresses her anger (her mother had coincidentally died shortly after Jyoti had felt angry with her). The imagery brought by group members concentrated for several weeks on death and violence. There were disclosures about forced abortions and molestations. Each woman began to make profound links between these disclosed events and their own feelings of revulsion at certain parts of their bodies. This led on to us dancing to reclaim those body parts. Eventually, one woman said that she intended to get measured properly for a brassière, for the first time in years. A poignant and important discovery by one group member around this time was that it had been easier for her to accept the pain of rape by a much older male relative than to admit to herself that her brother had also abused her, however gently. Once she accepted this, she was also able to accept her own gentler side.

Attachment and Mourning

The therapeutic relationship is fundamentally different from that of parent and child, although it does contain some elements of that relationship. The aspects it does not contain include the punitive/controlling functions of a parent, although certain boundaries are maintained. Neither is the therapeutic relationship likely to endure for as long or encompass such frequent contact as the parent–child relationship. The therapist is in a position, due to the boundaried nature of the work, to offer unconditional positive regard that might at times feel far superior to the love bestowed by one's parent. The ending of therapy is thus in some ways like the death of an ideal parent. Even when the client chooses to end, the ending when it comes can sometimes feel premature. Of course, this is not always the case. I have known myself (as client) sob out loud at the end of an intensive week of residential group therapy, and to breathe a sigh of relief at the end of much longer term individual therapy. It was not that my therapist had failed in her task, but perhaps that it was simply the right time. I had reached saturation point.

I find, therefore, that endings can be painful for my clients even after quite brief periods of therapy. At first, I wondered if this was because I was failing to work with and mobilise the individual's adult coping strategies. But when I think back to my clinical work with mothers and young children, I know that my instinct was to help them to bond before supporting the separation-individuation process (Mahler, 1979). This was important despite the child being a toddler who normally would be engaged in developing as an individual with a separate identity from that of the mother. I knew that it is impossible to move forward towards relative independence[1] (Winnicott, 1963) until attachments had been satisfactorily formed. I also know from my own experience of losing a parent that it is possible to move through the grief to a point of acknowledgement that my father lives on in some sense by being internalised by me. The way I am with my own children, the way I sit sometimes, even the way I cut up ingredients for a sandwich, will suddenly remind me of him and make me chuckle and cry all at the same time. I know I would not want to have missed this experience. And so, when my clients are in pain at the ending of therapy, I know that this is a necessary pain. I do not wish it on them, and I wish there was another way, but I know we cannot skip the painful bits and just jump forward. Healing and growth are lifelong events, reaching beyond the confines of formal therapy.

The Penultimate Crisis

I have observed in my clinical work that a crisis often emerges in the penultimate session. I have observed all of the following at some time or other:

- Parents avoiding dance time with their children.
- Demand for a social work assessment.
- Anger with me for leaving the client, like her lover who died.
- Anger with me for how much the client had changed and thus disturbed the *status quo*.
- Coughs and other physical illnesses.
- Worsening of mental health symptoms.
- Denial of the group's ending.
- Anxiety about housing.
- Having an affair despite the cementing of a relationship.
- Reports of money being stolen.
- Car accidents.

Many professionals would interpret this behaviour as 'acting out'. However, I believe this to be a pejorative and unwarranted judgement. Rather, I see these crises as cries for help as the individual comes to terms with their fear of loss of support. In most cases, the crisis resolves itself before the final session.

Of course, it is not only in the penultimate session that clients show us they are mourning a loss.

Shelley had fears of being touched. When she was a child her father described her as a 'delicate plant' and she now felt that if she was touched she would disintegrate. Just before our last session she had a minor car accident. She had also danced in a workshop with someone in a duet that did not feel pleasant, and sat in a tea-soaked chair. These were all unpleasant, jarring contact experiences, but she survived them. As we danced together in our last session, our toes playfully and softly encountered each other. As they slowly disengaged, I had the sense that this was a different kind of encounter, and a different kind of ending for her. She seemed more solid.

The Role of DMT in Processing Loss

I would like to give some examples of how my clients have made use of DMT in order to process their feelings of loss. Groups and individuals in therapy begin to work on issues to do with endings before the last session. Often their concerns will emerge within the movement metaphor.

Wendy attended the group session as usual. At the beginning, I mentioned that there would be just five more sessions after today. No one seemed particularly perturbed. However, when we started to move with the stretch cloth Wendy threw herself at it, allowing the group to support her as it contacted her waist and provided a secure yet flexible barrier. She repeated this movement a few times, and then said that the cloth (read group?) had stopped her from going over the edge. Someone else said he didn't know many people who had been to the edge. Wendy replied that she had been there, and didn't want to go there again. A large balloon was introduced, and the group bounced this up and down on the cloth for a while. After a while longer, I suggested that the group needed to find a way to end the movement. Sharon, who I knew heard voices telling her to harm either herself or others, instantly let the cloth drop, and the balloon with it. She remarked that the balloon had 'snuffed it'. The other group members then also let the cloth drop, one by one. Harry was the last, and he and I carefully folded it onto the ground. Later, in the verbal processing of this part of the session, Harry said 'What if there were no group?' I reminded him that this group would not be there forever, and we began to consider how that might feel and what the group members might do about those feelings.

What is fascinating about the above example is that Wendy was acutely psychotic, as were several people in the group. The richness of symbolism in people with psychosis, it seems to me, is not random but full of meaning. Moreover, it serves as a bridge for people whose psychotic symptoms might otherwise isolate them. Wendy's symbolism was understood by the other group members without the need to make this explicit and at the same time provided me with an opportunity to help the group to begin to process the ending.

In some cases, as in the following example, the loss of the group is compounded by other life transitions.

Agnes was leaving the group because a nursing home place had been found for her. She came to the group in tears, not wanting to leave. We danced in pairs within the group, using fans to mirror each other's movement. This re-affirming of her relatedness made her feel a little better. I had seen her progress in the group from a state of withdrawal, hunched over and not speaking. She now spoke lucidly, made eye contact and maintained an upright position. The total picture seemed to denote her readiness to engage with others.

It is a hard therapist who would not be moved by a client's deeply felt loss, and it is extremely important not to minimise the reality of people's lives. However, reminiscence can provide a bridge to happier times and an important relief from depression. In re-living better times within the creative milieu, it is possible to acknowledge that those healthy parts of the self and of society still exist in some form, as the following example demonstrates.

A theme emerged during one of our last sessions, of waltzing. One of the women in the group remarked that she used to love to waltz, but could no longer do so. So I structured a hand waltz with her. Another woman began singing:

> *When you and I were seventeen*
> *And life and love was new*
> *The world was just a field of dreams*
> *'Neath smiling skies of blue*
> *That golden spring when I was King*
> *And you my wonderful Queen*
> *Do you recall when love was all*
> *And we were seventeen?*

This led to other songs being sung in the group about being seventeen. My co-worker, an occupational therapist, noticed at that point that we were seventeen in number that day. We ended with a follow-my-leader circle, to the sounds of the Glenn Miller Band.

Sometimes, the particular movement forms or props used by the group to process endings are determined by repeating themes from previous group sessions. This is especially so when a particular movement ritual, for example a circle dance, has been used to mark the ending of sessions. In the following example, a prop had become a symbol for the group as an entity.

We moved each week with a large piece of elastic, whose ends had been tied to form a circle. The group members used this prop to lean against, to hold onto with varying degrees of commitment, and to contain them as they 'took the floor', sometimes alone, sometimes to try out new partnerships. At the end of the last session, we improvised with the elastic circle for one last time. The group, as always, was encouraged to find their own ending to the improvisation. Without speaking, they together began to place the elastic circle slowly and carefully on the ground. They stood in silence for a while, looking at it reverentially, before I said 'The session is over'.

Therapist-led Endings

In all of the above examples, the group as a whole found a way to end. Sometimes this is not possible, and the therapist has to take a more active role in helping individuals to process and come to terms with ending.

The group had been meeting specifically to work on themes of loss. One young woman had lost both her parents to cancer and was terrified that she might also die this way. Another woman had lost a son to suicide. A man had lost his first wife, and despite remarriage felt unable to move on. I decided to structure an improvisation around a party. We imagined the studio to be the venue, with a kitchen, food table, dance area, bathroom and bedroom for coats. I asked the members of the group to place themselves in the party, and interact or not in whatever way they chose, taking up positions in space that showed how they felt about being there. Then I suggested they find a time to leave. Would they go before everyone else? Would they wait to see when others were going and follow the rush? Would they wait until the dawn and be the last person there, chatting to the host? Afterwards, we discussed the relevance of this improvisation for each person's life, including their attitudes to the lost loved ones and to the ending of the group.

I sometimes suggest that group members throw or place down into the circle an image of what they would like to leave behind, and take something they would like to keep to help them on their future journey, or form and present a gift to someone else in the group.

At other times, I use a form of 'movement sculpting'. Group members are asked to place themselves in the room as they were at the beginning of therapy. They then move the journey of their therapy with its highs and lows, twists and turns, hiccups and absences, stasis and steps backwards as well as leaps forwards and so on. Eventually they arrive at the point where they are now. They look back and contemplate their journey so far, before taking a step into the future. When they have done this, they allow themselves to embody this experience, sensing how it is different from or follows on from the journey so far.

One particularly powerful way of ending a group is to use a ball of wool as a prop.

I held onto one end of the ball and gave the rest to Frankie. As I handed it to him and he sat back to hold it, I told him warmly about the time we had shared, when he had danced the dance of his ancestors. I said that in that moment I felt privileged to see where he had come from, that it was a real gift. He nodded sagely. Then, after a silent acknowledgement of each other, he held onto his end of the wool and gave the rest to Beryl. He told her memories of how he was moved to tears by the time she danced her way out of the labyrinth. And so it went. Each gave something to the other, in acknowledgement of how they had touched each other's hearts. At last, the wool was unwound. I remarked that now it was time to wind up the group. Silently, we passed the wool back and forth across the circle, in reverse order. We wound as we did so. Finally, the ball of wool again arrived with me. The group had been wound up.

In some cases, the structures I use are supplementary to the DMT itself, but equally important. For example, in work with families, I often take a polaroid photograph of the family in the first session for them to stick onto the front of their notes. This is repeated in the last session. Parents frequently remark on the differences in body posture, facial expression and proximity of family members. In adolescent or adult groups, we sometimes make celebration charters. Each group member has a large (A3) sheet of paper with their name at the top. Felt tips are available for group members to write anonymous, celebratory messages to each other. The charters can then be rolled up and presented to each member in turn, rather like a graduation ceremony.

Movement Profiles in the Ending Phase of DMT

In the previous two chapters, I have made reference to some observations from videotaped sessions of a DMT group with women. All of these women had been abused as children and had dependency issues that were getting in the way of them moving on from the mental health services. I now present my observations at the time of the group ending.

Anne moved for the last time in the penultimate session of the group. She did not know at the time that this would be her last opportunity to dance in the group. Transport difficulties meant that she arrived just in time for the verbal debriefing of the last session. Despite not knowing this would happen, she displayed some signs of separating from the group in the penultimate session, in that her movement became predominantly gestural (Lamb and Watson, 1979), with her lower body much more held than the upper part. She seemed to be holding something in. Her movements were very relational, in that they were performed on the table plane (emphasising the ability to reach out to others), but there was a resistance to the movement, or 'Bound Flow'. She was very aware of the whole group, offering her attention all around, as if she felt responsible for others despite needing to protect herself. I wrote about her in my observation notes that I felt a sense of remoteness, of her being in her own playful world. Her rhythms were a mixture of inner genital libidinal, like slowly undulating ocean waves, denoting pleasure, and oral aggressive, like the action of biting which is associated with separation (Kestenberg and Sossin, 1979).

Brenda, in the very last session, was also predominantly gestural in her movement. She seemed to be avoiding relating to the other member of the group or to the therapist, in that her movements lacked flow (North, 1972). She spent a lot of her time hitting a large physiotherapy ball with strength and focus. She hunched her shoulders as she did so and used a small kinesphere, or reach space, away from the centre of the body. She seemed to avoid moulding her actions into the prop, as if needing to protect herself from involvement with anything exterior to herself. However, her phrasing displayed a healthy balance between aggressive and nurturing aspects, in that she began each action with the force and directness and suddenness necessary to effectively hit a large object, but was able to allow the rebound and regain some control. The rhythm was decidedly oral aggressive (Kestenberg and Sossin, 1979), denoting a pre-occupation with separation issues.

Carol was in the same last session. Her body posture was sunken, associated with a depressive position. She also predominantly used gestural movement. She alternated between avoiding affective relationship to others (absence of the Flow Effort), and avoiding relationship to her self (absence of the Weight Effort). It seemed to me that she alternated between giving vent to her feelings and then being re-assuring, but that this was then followed by passivity and depression. The movement phrase in which this was evident was in her kicking the ball with little focus to the action, then retrieving it and holding it steady. She repeated this action several times, before retreating into a sunken stance.

The Developmental Process as Seen in Movement Observation

At the beginning of the group, Anne used rhythmic movement phrases that alternated between fighting and indulging. Her eye contact showed the same ambivalence. My sense of her was that she was dipping her toes in the water, then indulging in the joy of it.

By mid-way through the group, she displayed no such hesitancy. Making good use of all levels in space, my sense was of her taking in nurturance with strength, care and thoroughness, reaching out and gathering towards her from within the group, then holding and rocking in a carefully moulded way. She seemed firmly centred in her self.

Anne moved for the last time in the penultimate session of the group. As I explain above, she did not know at the time that this would be her last. Nevertheless, her predominantly gestural movement and use of oral sadistic rhythms perhaps signalled her sense of impending separation. Other aspects of her movement, including the addition of inner genital libidinal rhythms, suggested that she was indulging in the pleasure of her movement while she still could in this setting. She seemed to be holding something in, yet responsible to the group.

Brenda showed no hesitancy at all in taking in nourishment from the group and satisfying her dependency needs at the outset.

By mid-term Brenda seemed to be displaying a split between her upper and lower body. Her movements also showed impulsivity. My sense was of her withholding her anger in order to control it.

In the very last session, Brenda was still predominantly gestural in her movement. She seemed to be avoiding relating to the other member of the group or to the therapist, and showed signs of needing to protect herself from involvement with anything exterior to herself including a prop. However, her phrasing displayed an ability to recover from her aggressive expression with more nurturing movement. Her use of oral aggressive rhythm showed her preoccupation with separation issues.

Carol showed a clear split between the upper and lower portions of her body in her first session half-way through the programme. She also showed signs of withholding her emotions and little relationship to the group.

At the end, her sunken body posture showed that she might be depressed. She alternated between giving vent to her feelings and being reassuring, but this was followed by passivity and depression.

The Process Viewed as Whole

I am conscious that in presenting Chapters 3, 4 and 5 as separate considerations of the beginning, middle and end of DMT it might be possible to lose sight of the whole. I will therefore now share with the reader some complete, if abridged, case studies, that I hope show the threads between different stages in the DMT process.

The first case study shows how I adapted my style to work with someone for whom it was very important that she take control.

Sophie was a rape survivor. She was suffering from agoraphobia and had in the past both suffered an eating disorder and misused a non-prescribed drug. Her father had been rejecting, her mother controlling. Sophie described the women's self-help therapy she had been engaged in for her eating disorder as: 'We all crawled out of the woodwork with our mothers on our backs.' She told me that she had 'never taken a step to control (her) own life'. During assessment, Sophie made an image of herself on paper, in a baby walker.

Given Sophie's issues around control, I decided to offer her the opportunity to move unhindered in the space, with myself as witness.[2]

In her last session, Sophie decided to take with her the image of herself in the baby walker. She declared that she was now taking her first steps on this earth. She moved first on the spot, then began to explore what she wanted to gather up from the space to take with her, and what she wanted to release. As she did so, she was moved to gentle tears. I saw her touching the boundaries of the room, as if saying goodbye to an old friend. She then sank onto a floor cushion and held it to her. After a while, she formed a prayer-like gesture and then moved into what seemed reminiscent of the 'salute to the sun' in yoga. She looked strong and confident, grounded and flowing. Her movement didn't seem to need much verbal processing.

The following case example illustrates how coping strategies can work well until something of the nature of a crisis renders them useless. My way of working with Michael was deliberately structured, in order to appeal to his adult, professional coping self.

Michael had worked in security services and had witnessed a riot. He was diagnosed as suffering from post-traumatic stress disorder, and had been retired on medical grounds. He had some back problems following an attack at work, an arthritic foot, one leg longer than the other, and double vision plus central nervous system symptoms attributed to stress.

Michael told me that during the riots he had felt trapped, isolated and let down by management. As he described these feelings he held up his hands, palms presenting towards me, his body retreating as if backing into a corner. As we talked about him as a person, it emerged that he had a strong perfectionist streak.

There was some resonance between Michael's experience of the riots and his early experience. His father had abandoned his mother and five children. His mother had died when Michael, the youngest, was 21 years old and when her role as mother was effectively over.

When we examined Michael's movement metaphors during the assessment, he came up with: 'Put your back into it'; 'Lend a hand'; 'Pull your weight'. He seemed to be telling me about his concerns regarding responsibility and reliability. Towards the end of the assessment, he told me he feared he would let me down (if the therapy failed).

Together, we looked at Michael's feelings of anger at the system that he felt had let him down. These feelings had thus far been largely unexpressed, and he recognised that this meant he absorbed them. I asked him where in his body that absorption of unexpressed feelings occurred and Michael replied that this was his central nervous system. He made a movement like a shaking rag doll. Michael also at the same time had an image of rain coming at him at pressure, fatiguing him. I asked him what it would look like if he could release this pressure. He replied that he didn't know. I reminded him of his earlier gesture of palm presentation and retreat when talking about feeling trapped, isolated and let down by management. I suggested that we move in duet, holding two garden canes between our finger tips.

As we moved together, I noticed that he leaned heavily in my direction, so that the garden canes collapsed between our hands and he was forced to shift his position. I suggested flexibility in his trunk and forearms. He was able to respond to this suggestion, but found that his back hurt and he became weaker, like a rag doll.

Michael began to wear a lumbar support. He felt that his standards were slipping in his personal life. He mixed up his appointment times and arrived half an hour late one week. The day after the anniversary of the riots, he put his back out doing exercises recommended by the physiotherapist. This

113

necessitated attendance at the Accident and Emergency department of the hospital.

Eventually, Michael was able to make sense of the movement metaphors he had used. His movement began to use more flexible focus and shaping of the environment. This latter was graphically displayed as he told me he felt he had more control over his environment, making the gesture of hands on a car steering wheel. He told me as we ended that DMT had provided a bridge between his professional knowledge and use of nonverbal communication and his own body's way of speaking.

My next example shows the difficulties sometimes encountered in working with dancers whose training includes control over their body's expression.

Liz used dance as a form of escape. Her mother had tried to terminate the pregnancy when she was expecting Liz. Liz later suffered physical and emotional abuse, neglect and child sexual abuse. This included torture and forced prostitution. She had one older cousin who showed her some affection when she was little. The cousin was a dancer.

Liz felt that her whole life was like acting on a stage. I was struck by the resonance of her description with what Winnicott (1960b) calls the 'false self'. Liz felt that she was several different people, each with a different name, personality and way of moving. Although Liz had never been diagnosed as having dissociative identity disorder (American Psychiatric Association, 1994) this description of her difficulties is similar to the description of that particular diagnosis. Anecdotally, I knew the diagnosis to be used less often in Britain than in the US.

Liz initially placed me out of sight in the studio, round a small corner away from her. She spent the whole of our first session gradually moving towards me, making minimal eye contact. However, once having 'found me' she maintained very close proximity. Winnicott (1960b) describes the aetiology of the false self in terms of failures in dependency, and so it was no great surprise that Liz showed at first mistrust, followed by dependency behaviour. This continued in the dance movement, as she asked me to lead her movements. She implored me to come to a dance class with her outside of sessions and was devastated by my refusal to do so. She frequently tested the boundaries of the therapy by asking personal questions, usually after the session had ended. We worked together for two and a half years, during which time Liz slowly became more autonomous. However, when the therapy ended due to my pregnancy, she regressed and began self-harming. She told me I was like a mother to her, and it felt to her as if I were dying.

Of course, not all of the difficulties I had in working with Liz were due to her training as a dancer. Many people choose dance as a career because they want to gain mastery over their bodies. Clearly, Liz had good reason to want to do so and it is quite possible that formal dance had become her lifeline. However, the technical training requires very different skills from those associated with improvisation, which is the cornerstone of DMT.

Finally, I would like to present some family work, to illustrate the interrelationship of movement metaphor with family dynamics.

The family consisted of Megan, married to Jeremy, and their two children, Matthew aged five and Lauren aged two. Megan had had difficulties in bonding with her first child (Matthew), and had been referred to the mental health services following a diagnosis of depression by her General Practitioner. The care co-ordinator had decided that a referral to the Family Therapy Clinic would be useful. During their attendance at the Family Clinic, a referral was made to me for time-limited (20 session) family DMT.

During improvisations, I noticed that Megan tended to try to plan down to the last detail, before starting. In the first session, we were working with soft puppets. Matthew's crocodile attacked Megan's monkey. The crocodile said that it was cross and wanted to eat people. It said it felt bad because it was shouted at all the time. Jeremy said he was just looking on at all of this, and all he wanted was the family to be happy. Lauren sat quietly.

When they did dance together, Megan repeatedly grabbed Matthew's hands and encouraged him to jump up and down. Yet she avoided eye contact with him, facing him obliquely. The result was that he became excited and could not easily stop. When we discussed this pattern, Megan agreed that Matthew did tend to get easily excited, which had resulted in her avoiding play with him outside of sessions.

However, on one occasion we were playing a game of 'pass the gentle head stroke' around the circle. To my surprise, Megan recalled that she used to stroke her son's hair when he was a baby.

One of my beliefs is that in family work it is vital that I positively mirror the parents, using praise and whatever other tools are at my disposal. This, I feel, allows the parents to feel supported in their efforts to do the same for their children.

One of my most memorable sessions with the family was one in which the children decided to act out an episode of the British television series 'Thunderbirds'. The programme uses puppets and each episode is a variation on the theme of heroic rescue by the secret 'International Rescue' team. On this occasion, something or someone had fallen down a pit and needed rescuing. Megan decided to be the one in need of rescue, and Matthew was her rescuer. When I asked afterwards how this was like their family, Matthew said 'Mummy fell into a pit and had to call the Thunderbirds'. Megan quickly understood the metaphor, and said 'That's me, I'm in a pit and need help. I try to control things, but the more I try to control the more it slips away.'

In the last session, we watched a videotape of the family playing the same game but later in their therapy. This time, the parents were co-operating as the rescuers of their children. They had decided these roles for themselves. I remarked on the appropriateness of the progression from Megan being rescued by her son to both parents rescuing the children. After we watched the video, Matthew chose a sari cloth and talked about Chinese New Year. I produced ribbon wands, which became horns on the front of the dragon. The family also had fans to wave. At the end of their dragon dance, the family ended in a circle on the floor under the sari, as one peaceful and contained, self-nurturing uroboric (Jung, 1990) unit.

Evaluation and Looking Forward

What, if anything, do you feel you have been able to change in your life as a result of attending DMT?

What particular aspects of the DMT or of particular sessions did you feel helped you?

What else has been helpful in your life during this time?

What did you find uncomfortable or difficult about the DMT?

What in your life, if anything, has been unhelpful or got in the way of you making the most of your therapy since it started?

From your experience, what would you advise me to do differently in starting DMT with someone new?

What advice would you give to someone who is thinking of starting DMT?

What do you still need to work on?

Do you feel able to work on this without help from a therapist?

If not, what kind of help do you feel you need?

Do you have any other comments you wish to make?

Thank you for taking the time and trouble to complete this evaluation form.

Figure 5.1   *Evaluation Form for Clients*

Methods of research in DMT have been briefly discussed in Chapter 2. However, we do not need to employ full-blown research projects in order to evaluate our work and learn from it. One way to evaluate is to ask clients to complete a simple evaluation sheet (Figure 5.1). Clinical supervision also feeds into this evaluation process, employing the therapist's reflexivity to add to the client's testimony. Other more formal methods of evaluation include movement observation, CORE (Barkham et al., 2001) and the recording and analysis of notes. A full clinical summary in the form of a discharge letter to the referrer can employ any or all of these sources of information.

Evaluation of our work is essential if we want to be seen to employ evidence-based practice. This is especially important in the present British thrust towards clinical governance, but also makes good ethical sense. However, we must strive to ensure that our practice does not become diluted or ignored by an over-emphasis on randomised controlled trial research. Such research, valuable though it is in answering or beginning to answer questions to do with efficacy in relation to certain diagnoses, fails to do justice to the complexity of our art. Practice evolves through process research and in collaboration with service users.

Summary

In this final chapter of the book, I have examined the way that DMT can respond to endings. I have also given some more holistic overviews of the movement observation process and some complete case studies. I finished by considering the importance of a flexible but focussed approach to evidence-based practice.

Notes

1 More correctly viewed as 'interdependence' as Winnicott (1963: 84) suggests.
2 This was prior to me receiving any training in Authentic Movement™ and therefore was more influenced by my own experience of being witnessed by my teacher, Mary Fulkerson, during my dance training during the 1970s. A second influence would possibly have been the intensive workshops I attended with Dr Marcia Leventhal in the 1980s.

APPENDIX
USEFUL ADDRESSES

American Dance Therapy Association
2000 Century Plaza, Suite 108
Columbia, Maryland 21044
USA
Email: info@adta.org
Website: www.adta.org

APID Italian Promotion of Professional DMT
c/o V. Puxeddu, President
Via Principe Amedeo 13
Cagliari
Italy

The Association for Dance Movement Therapy (UK)
c/o Quaker Meeting House
Wedmore Vale
Bristol BS3 5HX
UK
Email: query@dmtuk.demon.co.uk
Website: www.dmtuk.demon.co.uk

Berufsverband der Tanztherapeutinnen Deutschlands (BTD)
c/o Silke von der Heyde, Chairperson
Benedikt Hagustr. 5c
80 689 Munich
Germany

Dance Therapy Association of Australia
18 Chatham Road
Canterbury
Victoria 3126
Australia

Dance Therapy Committee
Ann-Brit Tangstad
Nedre Berglia 72
1353 Baeruws Verk
Oslo
Norway
Email: tngstad@online.no

Finnish Dance Therapy Association
c/o Riita Parvia, Chairperson
Alveveien 45
N 9016 Tromso
Norway

The Swedish Association for Dance Therapy
c/o Birgitta Harkonen, Chairperson
Abrahamsbergsvagan 47, 2 tr
S-168 30 Bromma/Stockholm
Sweden

REFERENCES

Adler, J. (1996) 'The collective body', *American Journal of Dance Therapy* 18 (2), 81–94.

ADMT UK (Association for Dance Movement Therapy UK) (1997) 'Define dance movement therapy', *E-motion: ADMT UK Quarterly*, 9 (1), 17.

American Psychiatric Association (1994) *Diagnostic Criteria From DSM-1V*. Washington, DC: American Psychiatric Association.

Angus, L.E. and Rennie, D.L. (1989) 'Envisioning the representational world: the client's experience of metaphoric expression in psychotherapy', *Psychotherapy* 26 (3), 372–9.

Argyle, M. (1967, 1990) *The Psychology of Interpersonal Behaviour*, 1st and 4th edns. Harmondsworth and London: Penguin.

Balbernie, R. (2001) 'The effects of early experiences on brain development and long term implications'. Workshop given to the 7th professional conference of the United Kingdom Council for Psychotherapy: Revolutionary Connections: Psychotherapy and Neuroscience. Warwick University, 8.9.01.

Barkham, M., Margison, F., Leach, C., Lucock, M., Mellor-Clark, J., Evans, C., Benson, L. and McGrath, G. (2001) 'Service profiling and outcomes benchmarking using the CORE-OM: toward practice-based evidence in the psychological therapies', *Journal of Consulting and Clinical Psychology* 69 (2), 184–96.

Bartenieff, I., with Lewis, D. (1980) *Body Movement: Coping with the Environment*. London: Gordon and Breach.

Beck, A. (1978) *Beck Inventory*. Philadelphia: Center for Cognitive Therapy.

Beitchman, J.H., Zucker, K.J., Hood, J.E., da Costa, G.A., Akman, D. and Cassavia, E. (1992) 'A review of the long-term effects of child sexual abuse', *Child Abuse and Neglect*, 16, 101–18.

Bernstein, P. (1986) *Theoretical Approaches in Dance-Movement Therapy*. Volume 1, 2nd edn. Dubuque, Iowa: Kendall/Hunt.

Berrol, (1992) 'The neurophysiologic basis of the mind-body connection in dance/movement therapy', *American Journal of Dance Therapy*, 14 (1), 19–29.

Best, P. (1999) 'Improvised narratives: dancing between client and therapist', *E-motion ADMT Quarterly*, 11 (4), 17–26.

Billow, R.M. (1977) 'Metaphor: a review of the psychological literature', *Psychological Bulletin*, 84 (1), 81–92.

Blatt, J. (1991) 'Dance/movement therapy: inherent value of the creative process in psychotherapy', in G.D. Wilson (ed.), *Psychology and Performing Arts*. Amsterdam: Swets & Zeitlinger.

Boas, F. (1943) 'Psychological aspects in the practice and teaching of creative dance', *Journal of Aesthetics and Art Criticism*, 2, 3–20.

Brazelton, T., Koslowski, B. and Main, M. (1974) 'The origins of reciprocity: the early mother–infant interaction', in M. Lewis and L. Rosenblum (eds), *The Effect of the Infant on its Caregiver*. New York: Wiley-Interscience.

Browne, W.A.F. (1837) 'What asylums were, are and ought to be', reprinted in: A. Scull (ed.), (1991) *The Asylum as Utopia*. London: Tavistock/Routledge.

Carnegie UK Trust (1985) *Arts and Disabled People. The Attenborough Report of the Committee of Inquiry*. London: Bedford Square Press.

Carroll, M. (1996) *Counselling Supervision, Theory, Skills and Practice*. London: Cassell.

Chace, M. (1975) 'Dance alone is not enough', in H. Chaiklin (ed.), (1975) *Marian Chace: Her Papers*. ADTA. Originally printed in July 1964 *Dance Magazine*, 38, 46–47 and 58.

Chaiklin, S. and Schmais, C. (1979) 'The Chace approach to dance therapy', in P.L. Bernstein (ed.), *Eight Theoretical Approaches to Dance Movement Therapy*. Dubuque, Iowa: Kendall/Hunt.

Chodorow, J. (1991) *Dance Therapy and Depth Psychology*. London: Routledge.

Claid, E. (1977) 'Emilyn Claid talks to Bonnie Meekums and Kedzie Penfield', *New Dance*, 2, 10–11.

Cohen, B.B. (1980) 'Perceiving in action', Interview by Lisa Nelson and Nancy Stark-Smith. *Contact Quarterly*, Winter, 20–28.

Cohen, B.B. (1984) 'The developmental process underlying perceptual-motor integration', Interview by Lisa Nelson and Nancy Stark-Smith. *Contact Quarterly*, Spring/Summer, 24–39.

Condon, W. and Sander, L. (1974) 'Neonate movement is synchronized with adult speech: interactional participation and language acquisition', *Science (USA)*, 183, 99–101.

Cox, M. and Theilgaard, A. (1987, 1997) *Mutative Metaphors in Psychotherapy – The Aeolian Mode*. 1st and revised edns. London: Tavistock.

Cruz, R.F. and Sabers, D.L. (1998) Letter: Dance/movement therapy is more effective than previously reported. *The Arts in Psychotherapy*, 25 (2), 101–104.

Davidson, J.P. (1979) 'Ritual dance in Malysia', *New Dance*, 12, 4–5.

Dulicai, D. (1977) 'Nonverbal assessment of family systems: a preliminary study', *Art Psychotherapy*, 4, 55–68.

Ellis, R. (2001) 'Movement metaphor as mediator: a model of dance/movement therapy process', *The Arts in Psychotherapy*, 28 (3), 181–90.

Ernst, R., Rand, J.I. and Stevinson, C. (1998) 'Complementary therapies for depression: an overview', *Archives of General Psychiatry*, 55 (11), 1026–32.

Erwin-Grabner, T., Goodill, S.W., Hill, E.S. and Von Neida, K. (1999) 'Effectiveness of dance/movement therapy on reducing test anxiety', *American Journal of Dance Therapy*, 21 (1), 19–34.

Fogel (1977) 'Temporal organisation in mother-infant face-to-face interaction', in H.R. Schaffer (ed.), *Studies in Mother–Infant Interaction*. London: Academic Press.

Fulkerson, M. (1982) 'The move to stillness', *Dartington Theatre Papers*, 4th series, no. 10.

Fulkerson, M. (1987) Interview by Peter Hulton and Richard Allsopp. *New Dance*, 40, 20–21.

Gendlin, E. (1981) *Focusing*. London: Bantam.

Gill, D. (1979) 'Contact and change', *New Dance*, 12, 7–9.

Glaser, D. (2001) 'Child neglect and abuse: effects on the developing brain and therapeutic implications'. Keynote speech at the 7th Professional Conference of the United Kingdom Council for Psychotherapy: Revolutionary Connections: Psychotherapy and Neuroscience. Publication pending. 8 September, Warwick University.

Gordon, R. (1975) 'The creative process: self-expression and self-transendence', in S. Jennings (ed.), *Creative Therapy*. London: Pitman.

Gorelick, K. (1989) 'Rapprochement between the arts and psychotherapies: metaphor the mediator', *The Arts in Psychotherapy*, 16 (3), 149–55.

Green, A.H. (1993) 'Child sexual abuse: immediate and longterm effects and intervention', *Journal of American Academy of Child Adolescent Psychiatry*, 32 (5), 890–901.

Grenadier, S. (1995) 'The place wherein truth lies: an expressive therapy perspective on trauma, innocence and human nature', *The Arts in Psychotherapy*, 22 (5), 393–402.

Hackman, A. (1998) 'Working with images in clinical psychology', in A.S. Billock and M. Hersen (eds), *Comprehensive Clinical Psychology*, Vol. 6. Oxford: Elsevier.

Hadamard, J. (1954) *The Psychology of Invention in the Mathematical Field*. London: Dover Publications, Inc.

Hamilton, S. (1989) 'The dance of dementia', *Dice*, 9, 4–6.

Jennings, S. (1996) 'Brief dramatherapy: the healing power of the dramatized here and now', in A. Gersie (ed.), *Dramatic Approaches to Brief Therapy*. London: Jessica Kingsley.

Jones, P. (1996) *Drama as Therapy, Theatre as Living*. London: Routledge.

Jung, C.G. (1990) *Man and His Symbols*. London: Arkana.

Kane, E. (1989) *Recovering from Incest: Imagination and the Healing Process*. Boston: Sigo Press.

Kestenberg, J. and Buelte, A. (1977) 'Prevention, infant therapy, and the treatment of adults: 2. Mutual holding and holding oneself up', *International Journal of Psychoanalytic Psychotherapy*, 6, 369–96.

Kestenberg, J. and Sossin, M. (1979) *The Role of Movement Patterns in Development*, Vol. 2. New York: Dance Notation Bureau.

King, R. (1983) 'Dancing-Bodymind – a personal experience', *New Dance*, 26, 29–30.

Laban, R. (1971) 'The educational and therapeutic value of dance,' in L. Ullman (ed.), *Rudolph Laban Speaks About Movement and Dance*. Laban Art of Movement Guild. Originally published in 1959 in Laban Art of Movement Guild Magazine no. 22.

Lakoff, G. and Johnson, M. (1980) *Metaphors We Live By*. London: University of Chicago Press.

Lamb, W. (1965) *Posture and Gesture*. London: Duckworth.

Lamb, W. and Watson, E. (1979) *Body Code*. London: Routledge and Kegan Paul.

Leventhal, M. (1986) 'Dance movement therapy: Education or therapy' Part 2. *ADMT Newsletter*, 1 (15), 14–20.

Levy, F. (1992) *Dance/Movement Therapy: A Healing Art*. Revised edition. Reston, VA: American Alliance for Health, Physical Education, Recreation and Dance.

Lewis, P. (1984) 'The somatic countertransference: the inner pas de deux', in P. Lewis (ed.), *Theoretical Approaches in Dance-Movement Therapy*, Vol. 2. Dubuque, Iowa: Kendall/Hunt.

Lewis, P.P. (1988) 'Clinical focus: the transformative process within the imaginal realm', *The Arts in Psychotherapy*, 15 (4), 309–16.

Lewis Bernstein, P. (1986) 'Psychodynamic ego psychology in developmental Dance-Movement Therapy', in P. Lewis (ed.), *Theoretical Approaches in Dance-Movement Therapy*, Vol. 1. Revised edn. Dubuque, Iowa: Kendall/Hunt.

Low, K.G. and Ritter, M. (1998) Letter: Response to Cruz and Sabers. *The Arts in Psychotherapy*, 25 (2), 105–108.

Mahler, M. (1979) *The Selected Papers of Margaret Mahler*, Vol. 2. New York: Jason Aronson.

Malecka, M. (1981) 'Normal, once a week', *New Dance*, 20, 14–16.

Maslow, A. (1999) *Toward a Psychology of Being*, 3rd edn. Chichester: Wiley.

Meekums, B. (1977) 'Moving towards equilibrium', *New Dance*, 1, 8–10.

Meekums, B. (1988) *Dance Therapy in Family Social Work*. Leeds: East Leeds Family Service Unit.

Meekums, B. (1990) 'Dance movement therapy and the development of mother–child interaction', unpublished MPhil thesis, University of Manchester, Faculty of Education.

Meekums, B. (1991) 'Dance movement therapy with mothers and young children at risk of abuse', *The Arts in Psychotherapy*, 18 (3), 223–30.

Meekums, B. (1992) 'The Love Bugs: dance movement therapy in a Family Service Unit', in H. Payne (ed.), *Dance Movement Therapy: Theory and Practice*. London: Routledge.

Meekums, B. (1993) 'Research as an act of creation', in H. Payne (ed.), *Handbook of Inquiry in the Arts Therapies: One River, Many Currents*. London: Jessica Kingsley Publishers.

Meekums, B. (1998) 'Recovery from child sexual abuse trauma within an arts therapies programme for women', unpublished PhD thesis, University of Manchester, Faculty of Education.

Meekums, B. (1999) 'A creative model for recovery from child sexual abuse trauma', *The Arts in Psychotherapy*, 26 (4), 247–59.

Meekums, B. (2000) *Creative Group Therapy for Women Survivors of Child Sexual Abuse: Speaking the Unspeakable*. London: Jessica Kingsley.

Meier, W. (1997) 'The teacher and the therapist: different techniques and converging processes in the field of movement and dance', *E-motion ADMT UK Quarterly*, 9 (1), 8–10.

Moore, C-L. and Yamamoto, K. (1988) *Beyond Words: Movement Observation and Analysis*. London: Gordon and Breach.

North, M. (1972) *Personality Assessment Through Movement*. London: MacDonald and Evans.

Ostrov, K. (1981) 'A movement approach to the study of infant/caregiver communication during infant psychotherapy', *American Journal of Dance Therapy*, 4 (1), 25–41.

Paludan, M. (1977) 'Structuring body contact activities for children with learning disabilities: Part 1', *Contact Quarterly*, 3 (1), 6–10.

Payne, H. (1992) *Dance Movement Therapy: Theory and Practice*. London: Routledge.

Pedder, J.R. (1979) 'Transitional space in psychotherapy and theatre', *British Journal of Medical Psychology*, 52, 377–84.

Penfield, K. (1994) 'Nurturing the working therapist', *Association for Dance Movement Therapy Newsletter*, 6 (4), 4–5.

Poincaré, H. (1982) 'Mathematical creation', in H. Poincaré, *The Foundations of Science: Science and Hypothesis, The Value of Science, Science and Method*. Washington: University Press of America.

Prestidge, M. (1982) 'Nancy Topf: a question of personal development', *New Dance*, 22, 3–4.

Reich, W. (1962) *Character Analysis*, 3rd edn. New York: Noonday Press.

Ritter, M. and Low, K. (1996) 'Effects of dance/movement therapy: a meta-analysis', *The Arts in Psychotherapy*, 23 (3), 249–60.

Rogers, C. (1957) 'The necessary and sufficient conditions of therapeutic personality change', *Journal of Consulting Psychology*, 21 (2), 95–103.

Roth, G. (1990) *Maps to Ecstasy: Teachings of an Urban Shaman*. London: Mandala.

Ryle, A. (1990) *Cognitive Analytic Therapy: Active Participation in Change*. Chichester: Wiley.

Ryle, A. (1997) *Cognitive Analytic Therapy and Borderline Personality Disorder*. Chichester: Wiley.

Sandel, S. (1980) 'Countertransference stress in the treatment of schizophrenic patients', *American Journal of Dance Therapy*, 3 (2), 20–32.

Sandel, S. and Johnson, D. (1983) 'Structure and process of the nascent group: dance therapy with chronic patients', *Arts in Psychotherapy*, 10, 131–40.

Scarth, S.B. (1995) 'Supervision on the move', *Association for Dance Movement Therapy Newsletter*, 7 (2), 12.

Schaffer, (1977) *Mothering*. London: Open Books.

Scheflen, A. (1964) 'The significance of posture in communication systems', *Psychiatry*, 27, 316–24.

Schmais, C. (1985) 'Healing processes in group dance therapy', *American Journal of Dance Therapy*, 8, 17–36.

Schore, A. (1994) *Affect Regulation and the Origin of the Self: the Neurobiology of Emotional Development*. Hillsdale, NJ and Hove: Lawrence Erlbaum Associates.

Schore, A. (2001) 'Minds in the making: attachment, the self-organizing brain, and developmentally-oriented psychoanalytic psychotherapy', *British Journal of Psychotherapy*, 17 (3), 299–328.

Sherborne, V. (c.1984) *Sherborne and Movement*. Bristol Polytechnic Dept. of Education.

Shuttleworth, R. (1985) 'Metaphor in therapy', *Journal of Dramatherapy*, 8 (2), 8–18.

Silberman-Deihl, L.J. and Komisaruk, B.R. (1985) 'Treating psychogenic somatic disorders through body metphor', *American Journal of Dance Therapy*, 8, 37–45.

Sledge, W.H. (1977) 'The therapist's use of metaphor', *International Journal of Psychoanalytic Psychotherapy*, 6, 113–1178.

Sloboda, A. (2001) 'Music therapy with mentally disordered offenders', unpublished but taped lecture in the forum: Using the Arts Therapies – Finding Evidence to Promote their Practice. Chaired by Dr. R. Ellis. Royal College of Psychiatrists Annual Meeting: 2001, A Mind Odyssey: Science and Caring. London. 11.7.2001.

Solms, M. (1999) 'How does the talking cure work?', Video no. 9, *A Beginner's Guide to the Brain*. London: Anna Freud Centre.

Solway, A. (1988) 'New Midlands Dance', *New Dance*, 43, 12–14.

Spandler, H. (1996) *Who's Hurting Who? Young People, Self-Harm and Suicide*. Manchester: 42nd Street.

Standing Committee of Arts Therapies Professions (1989) *Artists and Arts Therapists: A brief Discussion of their Roles within Hospitals, Clinics, Special Schools and in the Community*. London: Standing Committee of Arts Therapies Professions.

Stanton-Jones, K. (1992) *An Introduction to Dance Movement Therapy in Psychiatry*. London: Routledge.

Steiner-Celebi, M. (1996) 'Aims of dance movement therapy', *ADMT Newsletter*, 8 (2), 11–12.

Stern, D. (1971) 'A micro-analysis of mother-infant interaction', *Journal of the American Academy of Child Psychiatry*, 10 (3), 501–16.

Stern, D. (1977) *The First Relatioship: Infant and Mother*. London: Open Books.

Todd, M.E. (1937) *The Thinking Body*. New York: Dance Horizons.

Trevarthen, C. (2001) 'Setting the scene: a window into childhood', keynote speech at the 7th Professional Conference of the United Kingdom Council for Psychotherapy: Revolutionary Connections: Psychotherapy and Neuroscience. Publication pending. 7 September, Warwick University.

Turnbull, O. (2001) 'Emotion and the neurobiology of false beliefs', keynote speech at the 7th Professional Conference of the United Kingdom Council for Psychotherapy: Revolutionary Connections: Psychotherapy and Neuroscience. Publication pending. 8 September, Warwick University.

Watt, D. (2001) 'Psychotherapy in the age of neuroscience: new opportunities in the renaissance of affective neuroscience', keynote speech at the 7th Professional Conference of the United Kingdom Council for Psychotherapy: Revolutionary Connections: Psychotherapy and Neuroscience. Publication pending. 8 September, Warwick University.

Webster, J. (1991) 'The use of the movement metaphor in movement therapy', in G.D. Wilson (ed.), *Psychology and Performing Arts*. Amsterdam: Swets & Zeitlinger.

Wilkins, P. (1995) 'A creative therapies model for the group supervision of counsellors', *British Journal of Guidance and Counselling*, 23 (2), 245–57.

Wilkins, P. (1999) *Psychodrama*. London: Sage.

Wilkins, P. (2000) 'Unconditional positive regard reconsidered', *British Journal of Guidance and Counselling*, 28 (1), 23–36.

Winnicott, D.W. (1958) 'The capacity to be alone', reprinted in: D.W. Winnicott (1987) *The Maturational Processes and the Facilitating Environment*. London: Hogarth Press.

Winnicott, D.W. (1960a) 'The theory of the parent-infant relationship', reprinted in D.W. Winnicott (1987) *The Maturational Processes and the Facilitating Environment*. London: Hogarth Press.

Winnicott, D.W (1960b) 'Ego distortion in terms of true and false self', reprinted in D.W. Winnicott (1987) *The Maturational Processes and the Facilitating Environment*. London: Hogarth Press.

Winnicott, D.W. (1962) 'Ego integration in child development', reprinted in: D.W. Winnicott (1987) *The Maturational Processes and the Facilitating Environment*. London: Hogarth Press.

Winnicott, D.W. (1963) 'From dependence towards independence in the development of the individual', reprinted in D.W. Winnicott (1987) *The Maturational Processes and the Facilitating Environment*. London: Hogarth Press.

Winnicott, D.W. (1971) *Playing and Reality*. London: Penguin.

INDEX